"A Book for People
Who Want to Become
Stinking Rich But
Aren't Quite Sure How"

By Benrik

D1342415

THIS
BOOK HAS
A DOUBLE
PURPOSE:

The first purpose is to provide the reader with a bright idea that may lift them out of middle-class wage slavery. Previous generations could settle for a quiet career and retirement, in exchange for not expecting to become rich. In the last few decades, that deal has collapsed – job security has vanished, steady careers are a thing of the past, and pensions are a scam. Paradoxically, the only way to stop worrying about money is to make lots of it.

The second point is to make capitalism itself more amusing. If we are going to live our whole lives under it, we may as well push it to its limits. It is after all just a mechanism, a tool to refashion the world to satisfy our wants, however surreal. We should not limit ourselves to the current repertoire, but should create products that inspire new, more exotic and imaginative wants – making the world around us more creative in turn.

The ideas in this book are deranged but plausible, if we enter into their unique logic. The reader is thus encouraged to pick one and go for it, or if none appeal, to use them to inspire their own project.

Good luck!

IDEAS

PRE-MIXED SALT & PEPPER

Each of us wastes hours of our precious time on this planet shaking salt and pepper separately onto our food. This may well be necessary for the fussy eater, but most people use them in roughly consistent proportions. Pre-mixing the two would save hours, and constitute a more practical, not to mention elegant, solution. Product range:

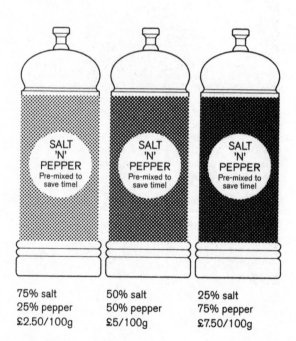

SALT
'N'
PEPPER
Pre-mixed to
save time!

SALT
'N'
PEPPER
Pre-mixed to
save time!

SALT
'N'
PEPPER
Pre-mixed to
save time!

75% salt
25% pepper
£2.50/100g

50% salt
50% pepper
£5/100g

25% salt
75% pepper
£7.50/100g

DREAM AGENCY

Many people have dreams to rival the greatest works of fiction. A "Dream Agency" would seek out the wildest dreamers and license their output to Hollywood studios so that they may translate it into "hit dream" blockbusters. Dreamers would visit www.dreamagency.com as soon as they wake up and file their latest dreams, to be vetted by readers for script potential. Sample high-concept dreams:

"The Man who Stole the Moon"

"Attack of the Cauliflower People"

"Elvis the gentle Nazi"

"The Adventures of Dudley the Cyborg Donkey"

"Dinosaur Incest: The Untold Tale"

Suitable dreams would be worked up into script form, with dreamers being paid a licence fee on any dream that is greenlit for production. Particularly fertile dreamers would be put on exclusive contracts and moved to L.A. where their sleep and dreaming could be monitored and exploited more scientifically.

Dream Agency commission: 10% of gross box office take.

JUNK FOOD HOME DELIVERY

Every self-respecting city dweller gets their box of organic fruit & veg delivered weekly from the countryside these days – but no one is providing the same service in reverse. Country folk should be able to order the very best junk food from urban junk-food providers. The service would effectively be the same: boxes would be delivered weekly to remote rural areas, along with a letter updating customers on the latest urban news, such as muggings, stabbings, etc., as well as tips on storing and reheating their junk food safely.

£15.99
+ £1 delivery

FAMILY BOX (Family of 4): 6 Quarterpounders, 4 Flame-grilled burgers, 6 Whoppers, 6 Chicken Whoppers, 8 McMuffin sandwiches, 14 portions of French Fries, Bucket of 26 McNuggets, 8 portions Onion Rings, 1 Triple Cheeseburger, 2 Regular Cheeseburgers, 2 Veggieburgers, Bucket of Coke (5l), Bucket of Diet Coke (3l), Bucket of milkshake (2l)

"SECOND YOUTH" SOCIAL NETWORK

In the wake of MySpace and other hugely successful online social networks, entrepreneurs are rushing to launch similar sites that cater to older age groups, where retirees can discuss pension plans, cruise ships and other clichés of old age. They are missing a huge opportunity: letting people relive their youth.

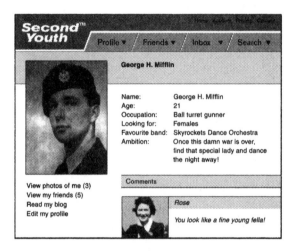

Second™ Youth

Profile ▼ / Friends ▼ / Inbox ▼ / Search ▼

George H. Mifflin

Name:	George H. Mifflin
Age:	21
Occupation:	Ball turret gunner
Looking for:	Females
Favourite band:	Skyrockets Dance Orchestra
Ambition:	Once this damn war is over, find that special lady and dance the night away!

View photos of me (3)
View my friends (5)
Read my blog
Edit my profile

Comments

Rose

You look like a fine young fella!

A "Second Youth" social network would encourage OAPs to post pictures of themselves from their twenties, listen to the music of their youth, brag about any wartime heroics, and flirt shamelessly with each other – just like the modern-day MySpace crowd. On the internet, you can be anyone – even yourself fifty years ago...

ART-SPONSORING ESTATE AGENCY

The process by which a neglected urban area becomes expensive is now well established:

1. Impoverished artists move in. Their presence makes the neglected urban area trendy.
2. Bars are opened. Features are written. Lofts are renovated. Advertising and City types move in. Property prices go through the roof.
3. Artists move out, and on to the next area.

A forward-looking estate agency could initiate the entire process by earmarking a potential area, and promising to buy work from any artist who established their studio there. Impoverished art students would flock to their new patron's neighbourhood, thereby sparking the cycle of trendification. The estate agency would make a killing by buying up local properties at the outset when they are still dirt cheap. It could also end up with a potentially priceless collection of art.

SAMARITANS LITE HELPLINE

The Samaritans provide an indispensable
service for anyone feeling suicidally depressed.
However, most depression is less acute.
A "Samaritans Lite" helpline would take calls
from people who merely wish to grumble about
life for 50p a minute. When you don't wish to
trouble your loved ones and acquaintances, or
when they have long since stopped listening to
you, you could call the helpline and be connected
to someone trained to moan with you.

Sample gripe	Trained answer
My wife doesn't understand me!	She doesn't deserve you.
This country is going to the dogs!	You're quite right, it's those immigrants, isn't it.
It's been raining all week!	Quite – my arthritis is playing up.
I'm stuck in traffic, I'm going to miss *Eastenders*!	The plot is thin at the moment anyway.
Why was Harry promoted? He's incompetent!	I never liked him.
At this rate, we're going to be relegated!	I blame the ref.
The cat's left a mess all over the carpet again!	I hate it when that happens.
I have a lump in my groin.	You're probably going to die.

AIRPORT PUBLIC X-RAY MACHINE

In the post-9/11 era, long airport queues for security screening are a fact of life. Instead of queuing morosely, passengers could ensure their own security – and keep themselves busy – by helping to scan luggage on a giant screen.

1 Person = 2 Eyes = Fallible   100 Persons = 200 Eyes = Foolproof

TERRORIST ITEMS TO LOOK OUT FOR: Explosives, Radioactive isotopes, WMD, Scalpels, Semi-automatic rifles, Guns, Shampoo, Harpoons, Axes, Hatchets, Lip gloss, Knives, Nail scissors, Swords, Truncheons, Tear gas, Pyrotechnical material, Ammunition, Suntan lotion, Fireworks, Saws, Rockets, Detonators, Fuses, Grenades, Mines, Inflammable gases, Non-inflammable gases, Toxic gases, Paint, Paint thinner, Toothpaste, Petrol, Methanol, Kerosene, Moisturiser, Camping stoves, Matches, Bleach powder, Poisonous substances, Hair spray, Infected blood, Deodorants, Fuel tanks, Corrosive substances, Mercury, Acids, Pathogenic germs, Rat poison, Water.

PRISON BREAKS

Many prisoners prefer prison to the outside world, with good reason: obeying a set of rules frees you from the burden of decision-making. Prison gives you time to think and respite from the chaos of choice that characterizes our society. "Prison breaks" would allow non-criminals to sample some of these benefits, with a few weeks' holiday in a genuine prison (albeit free of genuine inmates). Includes:

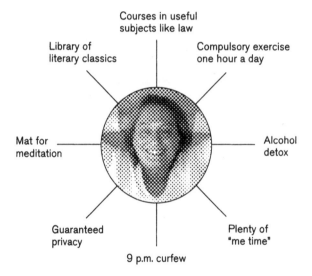

Courses in useful subjects like law

Library of literary classics

Compulsory exercise one hour a day

Mat for meditation

Alcohol detox

Guaranteed privacy

Plenty of "me time"

9 p.m. curfew

1 week	"War & Peace" package	£950
2 weeks	"Proust" package	£1,750
4 weeks	"Complete works of Charles Dickens" package	£3,100

RACE COACHING

As reality television has shown, it is entirely possible to be racist without knowing it. Indeed, being accused of racism comes second only to being accused of paedophilia in the hit parade of middle-class nightmares. To remedy this, why not start a "race coaching" company, which would help people purge themselves of their subconscious racism? Coaches would listen to their clients hold forth on race-related issues, then identify and correct their latent prejudices. Ethnic groups available:

White (British)
White (Irish)
White (Other)
Mixed (White & Black Caribbean)
Mixed (White & Black African)
Mixed (White & Asian)
Mixed (Other)
Asian (Indian)

Asian (Pakistani)
Asian (Bangladeshi)
Asian (Other)
Black (Caribbean)
Black (African)
Black (Other)
Chinese
Other

Suggested fee: £60 per weekly session with a bona fide member of a specified ethnic group, to include positive character testimonial if client is ever accused of racism.

ANTI-LOYALTY-CARD T-SHIRTS

The issue: These days, consumers are constantly pestered by supermarket checkout staff about whether they have a loyalty card. It would save time and aggravation on both sides if this could be established upfront.

The solution: Produce and sell a range of T-shirts that clarify the consumer's position at the checkout, thus avoiding pointless questions.

The market: The millions of consumers who decline to use a loyalty card for reasons of privacy, politics, or sheer bloody-mindedness.

BLACK-SKY THINKING

Consultancies make millions out of "blue-sky thinking" sessions with major corporations, where employees are encouraged to put awkward reality to one side and dream up lateral solutions to their business conundrums. Black-sky thinking would work on similar lines – except employees would be asked to think of horrendous, if unlikely, outcomes of their business decisions.

Blue sky	Black sky
"What if we could make a bicycle with just one wheel?"	"What if our bicycles' wheels both fell off at once, on the motorway?"
"What if we gave the new product away for free?"	"What if newborn babies turned out to be allergic to the new product?"
"What if customers could talk to the engineers directly?"	"What if disgruntled customers sued our engineers personally?"
"What would we make if the world became sunnier?"	"What would we make if humankind faced imminent extinction?"

Both methods would yield equally valid unexpected insights, but black-sky thinking is more in tune with our times, coaxing business breakthroughs out of chaos.

BLUETOOTH BLUE PLAQUES

Why not produce Bluetooth-equipped blue plaques, which house owners could stick on the wall and from which anyone strolling past with a mobile could download interesting information – who lives there, what they do, their vision of life, where they bought the sofa you can see through the window, which famous people they would invite in for tea.

"Bob was born in 1964 in Bristol. He moved to this house in 1982, and hasn't looked back! It was last redecorated in 2003, thanks to Bob's redundancy package from Johnson and Barker Ltd. (those arseholes)..."

It could also contain more practical information, such as instructions to the delivery man, or how much the owner would agree to sell the house for.

TRAUMA ART SCHOOL

Set up an art school that traumatises
pupils so profoundly that they have
enough material for a glittering career.

Ages 4–7: Society & Politics	– Parents' income embroidered on each child's uniform. – 10% fewer chairs than pupils. – Friendship punished by immediate expulsion.
Ages 8–11: Nature & Landscape	– Pupils to slaughter, gut and hang own meat. – Pupils to grow own vegetables in school field depleted by erosion. – School trip to oil slicks if available (swimming with parental consent).
Ages 12–15: Sexuality & The Body	– Mixed communal showers. – Pupils' favourite foods to be discreetly spiked with emetics. – Class photos to be taken naked.
Ages 16–18: Religion & Responsibility	– Pupils to be personally blamed for failure of Christ to return. – Pupils to be personally blamed for Shiite/Sunni split. – Pupils to be personally blamed for Dalai Lama exile.

Fees: 20% of pupils' future sales.

PERSONAL EXPLOSIVES-DETECTING DOGS

As everyone knows, these days terror can strike you anywhere, anytime and without warning. Unless, that is, you own a dog trained in advanced explosives detection. Animal trainers are now perfectly able to coach most dogs to detect explosives, but the science has never been applied to domestic pets, in spite of the obvious life-saving benefits.

The basic training would cover the main varieties of explosive on the market and cost £5,000 per dog. For that relatively affordable sum, the plain dog is transformed into a veritable bodyguard, capable of sniffing semtex at 50 feet and alerting its owner with a swift bark so that they may take cover.

There are 3 million dogs in the UK. If a mere 1% of security-conscious owners send their dog for training, it would yield a business with a turnover of £150,000,000 (30,000 x £5,000). There is also great scope for selling pre-trained dogs and for limited cat training.

WAITER BUZZER

Waiters make a habit of disappearing when
actually needed. The "Waiter Buzzer"
is a simple clip-on pager that diners give
to their waiter at the start of the meal.
They can then text the waiter from their
mobile with requests throughout the meal,
wherever he (or she) may be, thus saving
precious time on both ends and making
the restaurant-going experience stress-free.

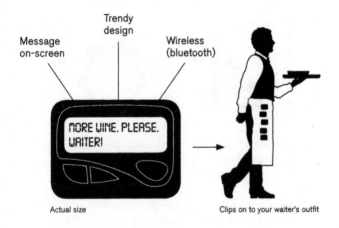

Message
on-screen

Trendy
design

Wireless
(bluetooth)

MORE WINE, PLEASE,
WAITER!

Actual size

Clips on to your waiter's outfit

Suggested price: £29.99 for basic version.
£39.99 for advanced (with loudspeaker
that allows you to talk to your waiter direct).

LITTLE TOE SURVIVAL KIT

Modern shoe-wearing civilization threatens the little toe with extinction. Already, most people's little toes are tiny, shrivelled up, barely mobile digits. Such are the forces of evolution that we seem to be inexorably heading for a world of webbed feet. "The Little Toe Survival Kit" would enable consumers to exercise their little toes, thus avoiding their disappearance. The kit would consist of a "Little Toe Separator" and instructions for correct use, as well as a full-colour scientific wall chart illustrating the anatomical processes involved, and explaining the work of Charles Darwin and other important theorists in the field.

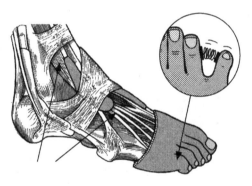

The LTS's spring-loaded piston technology would work the "extensis digitorum brevis" muscle, exerting an oblique movement on the interphalangeal joints and thus preventing synostosis (fusion) of the metatarsal bones.

Anyone who manufactured such a product would stand to make millions from those who are unhappy at the prospect of their descendants developing webbed toes. There is also vast potential for growth, by incorporating the LTS into a shoe range, for instance.

PERSONALISED BURGLAR ALARM

No one pays any attention to the monotonous ring of current alarms; they neither deter burglars, nor prompt neighbours to call the police. Personalised alarms would enable people to record their very own message to the thief, answerphone-style. From pleas ("Please don't burgle me, I've just been made redundant and my wife has dumped me!") to threats ("If I find you, I'm gonna cut your balls off and feed them to you through your nostrils!"), let your imaginative alarm message convince the burglar to leave your belongings in peace.

Examples for the car:

"The brakes are dodgy! The brakes are dodgy!"

"Stealing is a sin – don't you want to go to heaven?"

"Self-destruct in 10...9...8...7...6...5...4...3...2..."

Examples for the home:

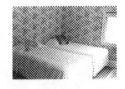

"Look, you can take the jewellery but please leave the TV, it's uninsured!"

"The next-door neighbours have much better stuff, and they leave their back door unlocked."

"Well done! You have walked into my pleasure dome, gimp-boy..."

PLACEBO PILLS

The "placebo effect" is a well-documented scientific fact: merely believing that you're being treated for illness helps you recover. Why not therefore launch a range of "Placebo" drugs, for headaches, sore tummies, colds and other psychosomatic illnesses? From a business point of view, the only costs are packaging, empty pills and a worldwide advertising campaign.

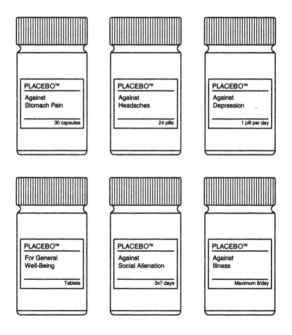

PLACEBO™
Against
Stomach Pain
30 capsules

PLACEBO™
Against
Headaches
24 pills

PLACEBO™
Against
Depression
1 pill per day

PLACEBO™
For General
Well-Being
Tablets

PLACEBO™
Against
Social Alienation
3x7 days

PLACEBO™
Against
Illness
Maximum 8/day

The market: over-the-counter self-medicators with psychosomatic and/or hypochondriac symptoms.*

*Global market estimated at $90bn in 2008 and growing fast.

TRAIN PARROTS TO SPEAK UNPALATABLE TRUTHS

Parrots have been unjustly appropriated by the pirate in popular imagination. Reclaim them for modern society by teaching them what we cannot say. Place them in a fancy art gallery for a couple of weeks and voilà, you have a commentary on freedom of speech and the limits of self-expression at the dawn of the third millenium.

Art is bankrupt!

No one knows what they're doing!

We live in a fascist state!

Down with the bourgeoisie!

Too late to stop global warming!

We're all gonna die!

How to: To train your bird, plan a half-hour elocution lesson per day. Make sure the TV is off and there are no other distractions, remove the parrot from his cage and prop him on your shoulder. Initially try to teach him simple phrases such as "Good morning" or "How are you?". He may only squeak in response to this in the beginning, but persevere, repeating the phrase, and you will eventually obtain results. Do not confuse the parrot with complicated clausal sentences at the outset, or he will lose heart. Be sure to give the parrot positive feedback, stroking his beak when he gets it right. It may take a few weeks for your buddy to learn its first word but once he is over this hurdle, the following words should come quickly. No swearing! That would be predictable.

Estimated price at auction: £12,000/parrot.

PRIVACY RETAIL CHAIN

The combination of post-9/11 paranoia and the spread of the internet is spawning a surveillance society so all-pervasive it would have made Orwell's jaw drop. In the physical world, CCTV cameras spy on our movements, police have increasing powers of detention without charge, and the convenient "terror threat" is invoked if anyone objects. In the virtual world, all our online activities are automatically logged by corporations that are subject to profit-making imperatives, and to government interference – hardly reassuring guardians of our most intimate secrets.

As the public becomes aware of the scale on which its privacy is being violated, there will be room for a privacy brand – perhaps a chain of cafés, or shopping malls, which will certify they do not capture any private data about you.

	– CCTV-free
	– Only cash accepted
	– No ID required
	– Anonymous wi-fi
	– GPS-jamming equipment

Other shops and hotels would also be able to apply for the Privacy Label, which would attract people who wish to get away from the intrusive 24/7 monitoring that increasingly blights our lives.

BONE TATTOOS

Normal tattoos fade with the years, as the skin ages and wrinkles. Bone tattoos would last for ever, surviving us to be read by future archaeologists. They would be more painful and expensive to undergo, and would therefore be suited only to the most important symbols or messages.

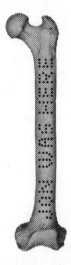

Procedure: The average bone tattoo would take a year to produce. An ultra-thin surgical needle would be inserted into the arm, far enough to make a little mark in the bone – under anaesthetic, of course. The marks would be added one a week, to allow for the swelling to subside.

Cost: £150 x 52 = £7,800 – a small price to pay for immortality.

CELEBRITY SPEAKING CLOCK

Now that most people's computers show the correct time via the internet, the speaking clock needs something extra to draw the crowds. Relevant celebrities would record their uniquely entertaining version in an appropriate tone; Jeremy Paxman would tell the time severely, for instance, or Jordan arousingly.

The Celebrity Speaking Clock: Listen to the correct time from your favourite celeb!

Example script (Gordon Ramsay): "Eight f**cking o'clock... It's now ten past eight you lazy bastards... at the third beep, it'll be eleven past eight so hurry the f*ck up... God you're useless..."

Pay them a 20% royalty out of the 0845 number £1/minute fee – and watch the cash roll in.

SMOKE-FREE BOOKS

Smoking in literature sets a deplorable example to the young. They are taught that smoking is evil, and yet it is rife in some of the greatest classics on the school curriculum. A range of educationally-sound, smoke-free versions could easily be put together, without doing too much violence to the originals, and sold to eager schools and parents. Example:

"Sherlock Holmes sat silent for a few minutes with his fingertips still pressed together, his legs stretched out in front of him and his gaze directed upwards to the ceiling. Then he took down from the rack the old and oily clay pipe, which was to him as a counsellor, and, having it, he leaned back in his chair, with the thick blue cloud-wreaths spinning up from him, and a look of infinite languor in his face."

"Sherlock Holmes sat silent for a few minutes with his fingertips still pressed together, his legs stretched out in front of him and his gaze directed upwards to the ceiling. Then he took down from the rack the item of fresh fruit, which was to him as a counsellor, and, having it, he leaned back in his chair, with the tasty vitamin-filled juices dribbling down his chin, and a look of infinite languor in his face."

SELF-DISCIPLINE
CREDIT CARDS

Credit cards are indispensable, but they also tempt us into unmoderated spending. Today's chip-equipped credit cards are intelligent: they can store information about our identity and our purchases.

They could be programmed to know our personal itemized monthly budgets and prevent us from exceeding them. Someone on a detox, for example, could set their off-licence spending limit to £20/month. When they try to buy more, the card would simply be refused.

PLASTIC SURGERY SCOUTS

Like model scouts, "plastic surgery scouts"
would keep an eye out for interesting prospects
on the street, although rather than looking for
fresh-faced beauties, they would try to sign up
people who could use plastic surgery.

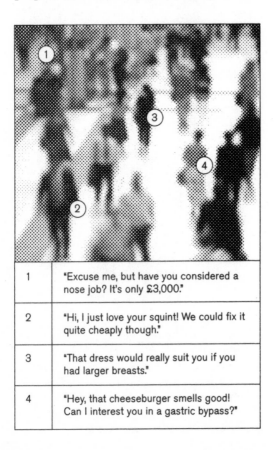

1	"Excuse me, but have you considered a nose job? It's only £3,000."
2	"Hi, I just love your squint! We could fix it quite cheaply though."
3	"That dress would really suit you if you had larger breasts."
4	"Hey, that cheeseburger smells good! Can I interest you in a gastric bypass?"

SAFETY COFFIN

There is a fate worse than death, and that fate is to be buried alive by mistake. Accidents do happen: there are many tales of desperate scratch marks found in coffins opened years after burial. The "safety coffin" would feature an emergency alarm button linked to the outside world, so that should the not-actually-dead emerge from unconsciousness, they can alert cemetery staff who will raise the alarm and disinter them.

Features:

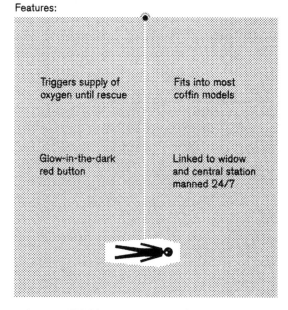

Triggers supply of oxygen until rescue

Fits into most coffin models

Glow-in-the-dark red button

Linked to widow and central station manned 24/7

Additional cost: £2,000 ("you can't take it with you")

TIARACAM

Newlywed couples are understandably keen to preserve the memory of their wedding day for posterity. Rather than have to trust some jobbing cameraman, why not let them capture every expensive detail exactly as they see it on the day? The Tiaracam is a stunning tiara fitted with a tiny digital camera that relays images to a lightweight hard drive, strapped beneath the wedding dress.

Available in a choice of settings:
Sapphire £3,500
Diamond £4,650
Ruby £1,100

The Tiaracam enables the couple to record a bride's eye view of the entire occasion, including walking down the aisle, the vows, the speeches, the first dance, and even – for the more adventurous couple – the first night!

ALSO! Groomcam: hidden in the buttonhole!

HOP-OFF AIRLINE

A "hop-off airline" would allow passengers to parachute off right above their destination. With the sophisticated GPS technology now available to travellers, they could simply enter their destination coordinates, and be warned by the hostess when they should get ready to bail out.

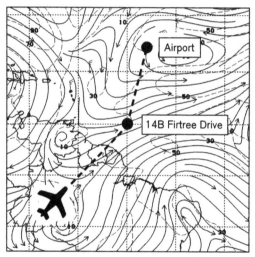

Time saving: 1hr37min

Of course, safety is paramount: passengers would need to undergo basic parachute training, but the expense would be more than recouped by savings on landing charges alone. Not only that, but many passengers would surely be prepared to pay a small premium for a swifter and more refreshing arrival.

CAR WITH MULTIPLE EMERGENCY BRAKES

Every car is now fitted with an emergency brake, in case the driver spots an unexpected split-second danger. This simple expedient saves thousands of lives a year. Why not manufacture a car that gives the passengers an emergency brake too? They are not busy driving the vehicle, and are thus freer to scan the road for threats. Eight eyes are better than two.

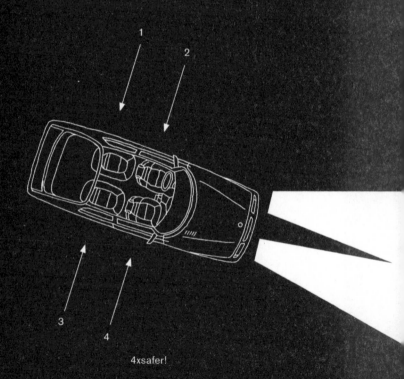

4xsafer!

FOOD POISONING TASTERS

We tend to take food safety for granted these days. Yet occasional scares such as those over salmonella or BSE, remind us that what we eat can potentially hurt or kill us. Indeed, it is estimated that 400,000 people are food-poisoned every year in the UK alone. An agency of modern-day food tasters would be certified by the Food Standards Agency and would offer their services to diners in fast-food outlets, in restaurant chains, or indeed anywhere where food is served. For 10% of the cost of each dish, they would taste people's food and report within five minutes on any adverse effects, enabling diners to enjoy their meal with total peace of mind. Cost of food tasting (examples):

— Big Mac 35p

— Soufflé 90p

— Mussels £1.20

— Duck à l'orange £1.50

Premium service: Food tasters were historically employed by rulers to protect against deliberate poisoning, of course. Thanks to recent developments, there is now once more a requirement for this level of service at the higher end of the market, in particular amongst rich Russian expatriates. A higher fee would be charged to match the higher risk.

DEFCON TEXT ALERTS

There can be few more urgent pieces of information than a change in the world's DEFCON status, which monitors how close we all are to nuclear annihilation. Yet no one has thought to make it available via mobile phones, which would give people more time to reach the nearest bunker, and thus increase survival rates.

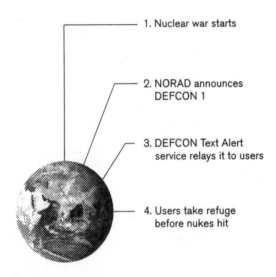

1. Nuclear war starts

2. NORAD announces DEFCON 1

3. DEFCON Text Alert service relays it to users

4. Users take refuge before nukes hit

DEFCON (defense readiness condition) is determined by the US Joint Chiefs of Staff at the Pentagon, in coordination with the President. There are five levels:

DEFCON 5	DEFCON 4	DEFCON 3	DEFCON 2	DEFCON 1
Peacetime (50p/text)	Heightened alert (£1/text)	Above-normal military readiness (£2/text)	Just below maximum readiness (£3/text)	War imminent (£7/text)

GOLFING SAFARIS

Golf and safaris are natural partners: both appeal to the love of the outdoors and the desire for physical activity; and both target competitive, affluent consumers. Golf's downside is that it can be too sedate and lacking in thrills. The safari's downside is that between the undoubted thrills, there is often not much to do other than wait for the animals to show up.

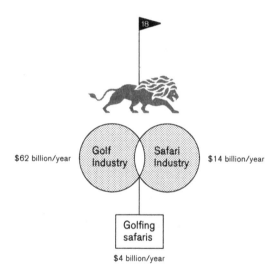

$62 billion/year — Golf Industry / Safari Industry — $14 billion/year

Golfing safaris — $4 billion/year

Golfing safaris offer the best of both worlds: doing 18 holes surrounded by wild animals – not since mammoth-hunting have skill and adrenalin been combined in such an exciting package.

Safety precautions: golfers must be careful not to hit the animals by mistake. Never take a shot if you do not have a clean line of sight. Do not drive near water if the animals are feeding. Wait until animals have left the green before putting. Do not leave any stray balls in the bush in case the animals choke on them. If in doubt, ask your armed safari guide.

SKULL PORTRAITS

Skulls are a beautiful yet poignant reminder of one's mortality: they lend any coffee table a cultured, Shakespearean air. Rather than any old dead person's skull though, why not provide personalised models, so that customers may purchase an exact replica of their unique skull.

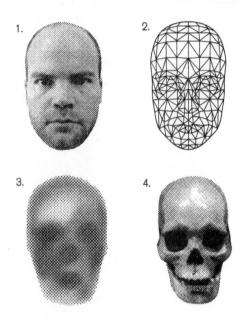

1. The customer's head is MRI-scanned.
2. The data is converted into a CAD model.
3. The skull is then constructed in photopolymers using rapid prototyping.
4. The customer can reflect on their very own mortality.

Suggested business suppliers:
Magnetic resonance scanning (MRI): www.vistadiagnostics.co.uk
Computer assisted design (CAD): www.polyimage.co.uk
Rapid prototyping: www.camodels.co.uk

BLACKMAIL PR AGENCY

A company can be made or unmade by word of mouth. There are PR agencies set up specifically to deal with "crisis communications" – to nip negative stories or rumours in the bud. No one has yet set up a PR agency to deliberately spread negative stories about brands, leveraging the speed and anonymity of the internet to destroy reputations. They could either demand payment from the bad-mouthed company to stop, or take payment from rival brands who would welcome the demise of their competitors.

BLACKMAIL PR
There is such a thing
as bad publicity...

KAMASUTRA FOR ONE

Everyone goes through a single patch at some point in their life. Why not help them make the most of it? The *Kamasutra For One* would research and teach the principles of advanced self-pleasure, principles that will turn anyone into a red-hot self-lover... Contents:

Men:

- The Angry Scorpion
- The Slack-Necked Giraffe
- The Serpent Spews His Venom
- Vishnu Tamed
- Polishing The Bamboo
- The One-Eyed Billygoat
- The Cobra's Hood

Women:

- Splitting The Mango
- The Infinite Yawning
- Calcutta (The Black Hole)
- Strumming The Sitar
- The Sugar Cane Root
- The Blooming Of The Lotus
- The Chapati Rises

To be beautifully illustrated in full-colour in traditional Indian style. Promote to the singles market on Valentine's Day.

BLOG GHOSTWRITING

Millions of people start blogs every year, only to abandon them when they realize just how much work is involved. Blog ghostwriters could take over the job for a fee. They would catch up with the nominal blogger for a few minutes every morning, then translate their thoughts and experiences into riveting prose that makes them seem fascinating, and wins them the admiration of friends and total strangers alike.

Self-written:
Had row with Mum. What a cow. Laters.

Ghostwritten:
Mothers are truly a mixed blessing. Whilst one is grateful to have been born, there are occasions (and this morning, dear reader, proved to be one of them!) where one might wish they displayed a less bovine disposition. Thus begins our tale...

Packages (per week):		
Basic	Blog relating average life.	£10
Advanced	Blog sprucing up average life with literary allusions.	£15
Premium	Blog making one's life read like a novel and leading to Hollywood studios competing to remake it as a movie.	£50

VIRTUAL DJs

Hiring a disc jockey for a party can cost
hundreds of pounds – even more for a
wedding. A "Virtual DJ" service would
provide DJs based in developing countries,
where manpower is cheap. For £50, the
Virtual DJ would mix the latest tracks,
take requests live by email, keep an eye
on the dance floor via webcams, and
deliver personalized "shout-outs" to the
party-goers to a pre-agreed schedule.

The skilled "virtual DJ" will be able to
handle up to six events simultaneously
around the world, boosting productivity
and thus "pumping up" the bottom line.
This is an opportunity to start the first
global party corporation.

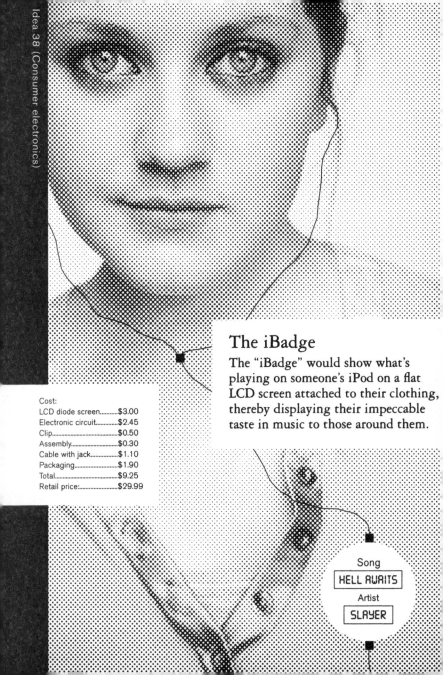

The iBadge

The "iBadge" would show what's playing on someone's iPod on a flat LCD screen attached to their clothing, thereby displaying their impeccable taste in music to those around them.

Cost:

LCD diode screen	$3.00
Electronic circuit	$2.45
Clip	$0.50
Assembly	$0.30
Cable with jack	$1.10
Packaging	$1.90
Total	$9.25
Retail price:	$29.99

Song

HELL AWAITS

Artist

SLAYER

ADVERTISER-FUNDED GOVERNMENT

If someone catches the media's eye these days, by having sex with a top politician or surviving an air crash, they are usually able to profit by selling their story. After all, if they create compelling news the media makes more advertising revenue, so why shouldn't they get their fair share? The principle could be applied on a much wider scale, by a news channel that rewarded governments whose actions caused a spike in viewers. In exchange for sharing 50% of advertising profits with the governments, the channel would get exclusive warnings of impending decisions, cabinet reshuffles, declarations of war and so on, enabling them to attract even more viewers.

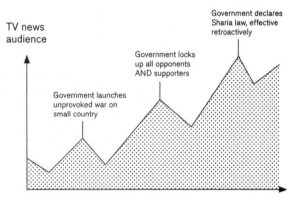

Profit share to government: £950 million!

Governments would also have an incentive to act ever more entertainingly, which would strengthen interest in the democratic process.

CHARACTER ASSASSINS

Becoming a fully-fledged assassin is illegal, risky and takes years of elaborate training. By contrast, becoming a professional "character assassin" would be easy, less dangerous and highly lucrative. A "character assassin" would be paid to destroy their victim's reputation. Techniques:

1	Stuff victim's letterbox full of copies of "Bondage Weekly"
2	Plant bloodied plastic sheeting in victim's recycling bin
3	Train local dogs to howl at victim's odour
4	Make local kids cross the road on sight of victim
5	Wink knowingly at local shopkeepers as victim walks past
6	Decorate victim's front door with garlic
7	Send dead flowers to victim at their workplace

MYSTERY TOURISTS

Using the same methods as "mystery shoppers", "mystery tourists" would assess whole countries incognito. At the end of their trip, they would produce a full report for the country's government on how to make it a more attractive tourist destination. The "mystery tourists" would provide the country with a comprehensive guide to a visitor's experience, from difficulties obtaining visas, to the state of the public toilets – feedback worth millions of pounds in increased tourist numbers! Sample report extract:

	China
Bureaucracy	"Customs official Shi-Ming Tsai at Beijing Airport let me through without checking my bag properly; I could have been carrying drugs and/or weapons."
Food	"High quality overall. Suggest change to more practical knife-and-fork cutlery?"
Safety	"9/10 for police presence on the beat, very reassuring for the foreign visitor!"
Landmarks	"Great Wall: mostly in good condition, unsightly pile of rubbish near Km 8 though."
Hospitality	"Extremely rude citizen, please have a word about her attitude (works in Shanghai Isetan department store, aged about 20, green T-shirt, glasses)."

CELEBRITY-WORN UNDERWEAR

The ultimate in exclusive chic: Underwear that has actually been worn by the stars of today. As close as most will ever get to the icons of our era...

As worn by... Kate Moss

As worn by... Brad Pitt

Business model: Assuming a 10-second time frame for the celebrity to put on and remove each individual item, estimated production could reach 2,500 units a day. At a proposed retail price of $400 for an A-list star, that yields a turnover of $1,000,000 a day, or $365,000,000 a year per celeb.

Includes guaranteed certificate of wear by the star!

CLEANER MARKETING

Who is better informed about a household's shopping requirements than the cleaner? Indeed, they probably know what consumer goods need replacing better than their employer: their very job is to go through people's belongings systematically.

Cleaner report:	Marketing action:
Husband needs new blue shirt (collar frayed)	Post shirt mail-order catalogue
Cat doesn't eat current cat food brand (Whiskas)	Post free Sheba sample
DVD player broken	Email 10% discount for online order
Husband plays golf	Post free 2-month trial of Golfing Weekly
She is reading Captain Corelli's Mandolin	Call with details of holidays in Greece

Solution 1: the cleaner could discreetly pass this information on to marketeers for a fee, enabling them to target the household with highly relevant marketing mail.

Solution 2: a marketing agency could subsidize people's cleaners in exchange for the data. Consumers could therefore get a) marketing info they actually need and b) £3/hour cleaning.

COMMUNIST SOCIAL NETWORKING SITE

By a strange quirk of history, communism was finally discredited in 1989 with the fall of the Berlin Wall, just a few months before the creation of the World Wide Web, in 1990. In many ways, the two would have been ideally suited:

GLOBAL
The internet is by its very nature international, and could facilitate the goal of worldwide revolution and the decline of reactionary nationalistic allegiances.

EGALITARIAN
Class distinctions count for nothing online.

www. **.com**

MATHEMATICAL
One of the obstacles to successful central planning was the lack of reliable economic data. Websites now collect this every time we go online.

VIRAL
The World Wide Web allows the immediate transmission of radical ideas, largely beyond the reach of ruling-class censorship.

PROGRESSIVE
Convenient and secure payment facilities such as PayPal make the redistribution of wealth painless.

The internet was born of capitalism, but paradoxically may enable more collective and authoritarian governance. The business model here relies largely on reaping the spoils of world revolution.

MOOD RADIO STATIONS

Now that radio can be broadcast digitally over the internet, with no need for expensive licences, powerful transmitting equipment and so on, there is much more scope for niche stations. "Mood radio stations" would provide a stream of music that suited your desired mood, reinforcing it or changing it if need be. For instance:

Angry
Fight the Power Public Enemy
The Prisoner Iron Maiden
White America Eminem
Injustice for All Metallica
Smells Like Teen Spirit Nirvana

Horny
Horny Mousse T
You Sexy Thing Hot Chocolate
Sex Machine James Brown
Touch Me Samantha Fox
Push It Salt'n'Pepa

Sad
Everybody Hurts REM
Crying Roy Orbison
Yesterday The Beatles
Tears in Heaven Eric Clapton
Send in the Clowns Frank Sinatra

Happy
Dancing Queen Abba
Beautiful Day U2
Freedom Aretha Franklin
Celebration Kool and the Gang
La Bamba Los Lobos

Other programming could also be adapted, with only good news being reported for example. Uplifting brands like orange juice would advertise on the happier stations, while insurance and other downbeat brands would get high response rates on the gloomier ones.

HELIUM-LINED SUITCASES

As helium is lighter than air, a suitcase lined
with helium-filled compartments would be
easier to lift. Its lighter buoyancy properties
are already used in airships. It would be
a fairly straightforward engineering task
to incorporate it into luggage, or indeed
to manufacture helium ballast sleeves that
one could pack into traditional suitcases.

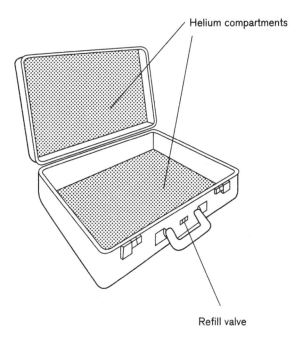

Helium compartments

Refill valve

Further research: see *The Encyclopedia of the Chemical Elements*, Clifford
A. Hampel (ed), "Helium" entry by L. W. Brandt (New York, Reinhold, 1968)

CONTINGENCY CAPITALISM

The greatest fortunes are made in times of sudden upheaval, when unforeseen events spin the world on its axis and reverse the cosmic order of things. The improbable happens again and again, so why not be prepared to take advantage of it? A "contingency capitalism" investment firm would fund businesses prepared to make money out of the totally unexpected, seizing new opportunities well before anyone else. Where an average venture capitalist normally looks for a x10 return, these businesses could generate x1000.

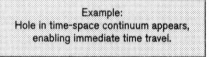

Example:
Hole in time-space continuum appears, enabling immediate time travel.

"Contingency Capitalist Fund"

Will have historically-trained mercenaries ready to travel back with exact locations of oil reserves, in order to secure them on the cheap before anyone else in history.

Will have brochures pre-printed to secure the lucrative and educational "holiday-in-time" market (including "Dinosaur Delights", "French Revolution" and "Burning of the Witches" packages).

Will have volunteers already primed to travel to the future and return with advanced technologies for commercial exploitation e.g. teleportation.

Other potential contingencies: Alien landing (peaceful/non-peaceful), return of Christ, return of Elvis, meteorite discovered heading for Earth within two weeks, red button pressed by mistake.

BEDSTORE HOTELS

Buying a new bed is tricky. It is difficult to judge it simply by flopping on it in the store for a few minutes. And yet your decision will stay with you for years, if not decades.

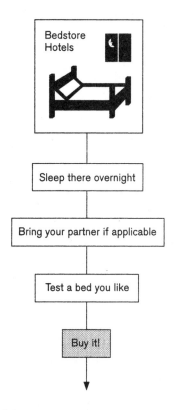

Potential market:
1 million beds bought every year in the UK x average cost £500......£500 million
1 million hotel nights x average cost £100......................................£100 million
Turnover:...£600 million

ANTI-THEFT MOBILE DOWNLOAD

Mobile-phone theft is a chronic problem, with a phone being stolen every 12 seconds on average in the UK, at a cost of £390 million per year. On top of that, by the time the phone is deactivated, the thief may have made thousands of pounds' worth of calls. The "anti-theft mobile download" would be triggered remotely by calling the mobile if it gets stolen, and entering a special code.

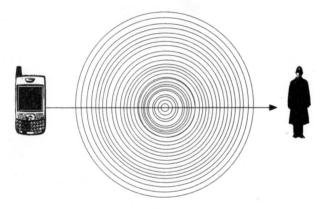

This triggers the phone to screech "Thief! Thief! Thief! You bastard! Thief! Stop him! Thief! Police! Help!" at 90 decibels, on a loop. The phone also locks so that the thief cannot switch it off, and has no option but to abandon it to be recovered by local police. Future versions may include electrocution facility, subject to technical agreement with manufacturers and health and safety compliance review.

NON-CELEBRITY LOOKALIKES

Celebrity lookalike agencies make a fortune by providing David Beckhams or Paris Hiltons for parties, corporate events and supermarket openings. Why confine this valuable service to the celebrity world? Everyone needs a lookalike to stand in for them at some point. Using existing facial recognition technology, it would be entirely possible to match anyone's photo to a lookalike online, and then hire the lookalike for the desired purpose.

Taking your place at a distant relative's funeral £100	"He will be missed"
During jury service £80/day	"Guilty!"
Passing your driving test £500 (qualified driver) £5 (non-driver)	"Oops!" **PRANG!**
Breaking up with your partner £50	"It's not you it's me"

HOME PRISON SERVICE

UK prisons are chronically overcrowded. With the Home Office paying close to £30,000 a year per prisoner, people could make money by turning a spare room in their house into a maximum-security facility. A "Home Prisons Service" company would recruit householders with suitable spare rooms, equip them with adequate security as per the diagram below, and supervise them to ensure prisoners' rights are respected at all times.

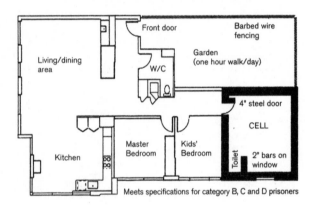

Meets specifications for category B, C and D prisoners

Annual budget:
Home Office payment:............................£30,000
Cost of special locks, reinforced
door and windows, panic button:.............£6,500
Cost of food:...£3,650

Profit...£19,850

To be shared between the householder and the "Home Prisons Service" company.

TALKING UMBRELLA

The market: 500 million umbrellas sold worldwide (2005-06). Worldwide rainfall: 6,500,000,000,000 mm (annual average). The target: People who don't notice it has stopped raining, thus needlessly holding up their umbrella.

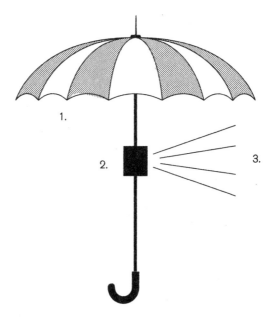

1. Sensors on the ribs detect degree of humidity
2. After one minute of non-rain, signal is transmitted to mini piezo speaker
3. Message on a loop: "The rain has now stopped. Please close your umbrella. The rain has now stopped. Please close your umbrella."

PERSONAL STOCKPILING

Our world is running out of natural resources – most of the wars of the 21st century will be over shortages of essential commodities. Already, the UK has seen supplies of fuel interrupted, and spates of panic-buying – so far on a small scale. There is a clear gap in the market for "personal stockpiling": buying a personal supply of water, fuel, gas and other key goods that we take for granted but can't do without. This would be kept in a secure location and released to its owners in case of social meltdown.

"Property of Mr and Mrs Bloggs. Keep out!"

Water	4,500 litres	£5
Fuel	80 gallons	£480
Gas	30,000 cubic feet	£165
Gold	1kg minted bar	£12,500
Total		£13,150
Storage fee		£650 (5%/year)

WEATHER-CONTROLLED ALARM CLOCK

This alarm clock would be linked to an outside remote weather sensor. The alarm would be set to wake you up if the weather is nice, or let you sleep in if the weather is foul.

£39.99. Perfect for weekends, retired folk and students!

EGO BILLBOARDS

Nothing beats the movie-star experience of seeing your face projected six feet high in front of hundreds. "Ego billboards" would make this easy and affordable. Tourists and wannabes would enter a modified photobooth, pay £5, and their face would be beamed up to a giant electronic billboard for one whole minute for all to admire.

"Ego booth" fitted with live camera...

...transmits to electronic billboard

Business model: media companies charge £1 million per year for a billboard on Piccadilly Circus. You would sell it on at £5 for 1 minute, yielding a turnover of £2.5 million.

Other potential sites: Times Square (New York), Shibuya (Tokyo).

SEX RED-LETTER DAYS

"Red-letter days" organize memorable experiences, like parachuting, go-karting, hot-air ballooning etc. But so far no one has created the equivalent for sex: extravagant sexual experiences that would be difficult to organize without third-party help — if only to keep an eye out for people walking in on the act. Couples would book each other Sex Red-Letter Days to spice up their sex life, particularly on Valentine's Day.

On top of a double-decker bus during rush hour	£150
In a skyscraper lift	£180
On a submarine one mile under	£740
On a FTSE 100 boardroom table	£210
With a porn star on hand to improve your technique	£530
With a jazz band following your rhythm	£350
Amongst the penguins at London Zoo	£190
In a haystack pre-inspected for rodents	£80

WILL-WRITING PEN

Making a will is a tedious and bureaucratic procedure, which is why only 41% of adults in the UK have an up-to-date one*. A product that might help would be a legally recognized, invisible ink "will pen"**: you would use it to write on your possessions, indicating whom they should go to in the event of your death.

To my bro Jason – drive safe!

To Auntie Rita

To my boss Barry – I slept with your missus in this haha only joking!

To my long-suffering wife

* Law Society, 2006. ** Police already use such pens to reunite stolen goods with their owners – they are visible under ultraviolet lights.

HEROISM FACILITATORS

These days, it is very difficult for a father to be a hero to his kids; modern society offers few opportunities to prove one's masculine mettle. A "heroism-facilitating" company would help by staging heroic scenarios, at pre-arranged times. Possible scenarios:

"The heart attack"	Dad brings the victim back from death's door with his instinctive grasp of resuscitation techniques.
	£350 (includes one victim + two bystanders)
"Cat stuck up a tree"	Dad bravely climbs up the mildly high tree to rescue the meowing moggie, to the frail little old lady's tearful relief.
	£450 (includes frail little old lady + trained cat)
"The mugger"	Dad witnesses a lady's handbag being snatched – he chases the mugger round the corner, returning with the handbag and a light bruise.
	£600 (includes lady, mugger, make-up artist)

Perfect for a Father's Day outing! Guarantees lifelong respect from impressionable kids. Do not exceed one scenario per year. Not for use on cynical teenagers.

PREMIUM AD BREAKS

TV viewers skip advertising breaks because they know from experience that most ads are rubbish. As a result, the few ads that are actually entertaining get a lower audience than they deserve. "Premium ad breaks" would only contain the best ads, and would announce this upfront so that more viewers might watch them rather than go and make tea or feed the cat.

Ads to be selected for quality by an independent panel
Good ads to get more viewers
Viewers to look forward to the "premium ad breaks"!
"Premium ad break" company would buy the media spots from TV channels, and resell them at a 20% mark-up

SPACE STATUES

Art on earth is subject to decay and eventual oblivion. Even the *Mona Lisa* will one day fade beyond repair. For true immortality, we must look to the stars. For a relatively accessible sum, the modern patron of the arts could have a statue of him or herself blasted into outer space, to journey to infinity and beyond.

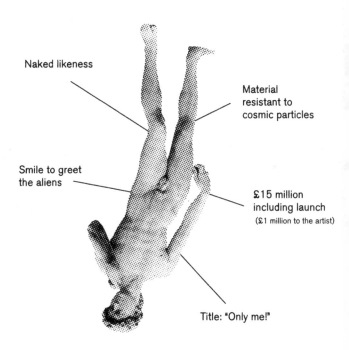

Naked likeness

Material resistant to cosmic particles

Smile to greet the aliens

£15 million including launch
(£1 million to the artist)

Title: "Only me!"

Perfect for the average Renaissance billionaire.

DECORATIVE BARBED WIRE

The rich spend millions building and decorating their magnificent homes, then ruin the overall effect by bedecking their outer walls with ugly Gestapo-style barbed wire. It would be quite feasible to produce a functional yet aesthetically-pleasing version.

Razor points arranged in natural rose thorn pattern

Available in a range of bright colours (yellow, orange, pink)

Electrified wire also powers contemporary lighting

Easy to bend into creative shapes

For the security-conscious yet discerning home owner: barbed wire that makes a statement.

AMATEUR LAW FIRM

Fully-qualified lawyers are prohibitively expensive. Yet thousands of citizens have picked up the legal basics from watching procedural legal TV shows, such as *Judge John Deed* or *L.A. Law*. Why not let them display their skills by representing claimants for a reduced fee.

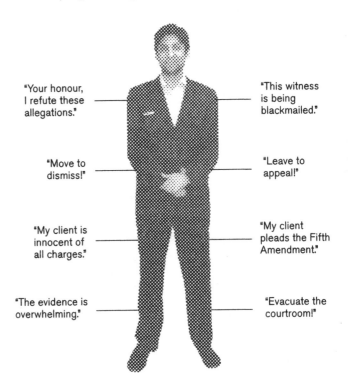

"Your honour, I refute these allegations."

"This witness is being blackmailed."

"Move to dismiss!"

"Leave to appeal!"

"My client is innocent of all charges."

"My client pleads the Fifth Amendment."

"The evidence is overwhelming."

"Evacuate the courtroom!"

The more gifted amateurs could progress to the bar, the poorer sections of society would gain a legal voice, and justice would be served all round.

Amateur lawyer (vetted by the law firm): £40/hour. Professional lawyer: £400/hour

COMMUTER SPEED-DATING

Commuters spend hours a day stuck on the train or the tube, bored witless. Many of them are young, single and time-poor. Designated speed-dating carriages would lighten up their journey considerably, and may help many find true love. How it works:

£1 entrance fee

One speed-dating carriage per train

Women sit on the left, men on the right

Chat to person opposite for one stop, then move on to the next

No body contact (except during rush hour)

Sponsored by romantic brand e.g. Interflora.

CAR REBRANDING WORKSHOPS

The most distinguishing feature of a car is often the badge. Most consumers cannot afford the more expensive car brands, such as Mercedes. A chain of rebranding workshops would source second-hand luxury car badges from eBay, and affix them professionally to people's cheaper cars, saving them thousands.

Before:

After:

Legal note: It would obviously be a violation of trademark law to sell a rebranded car. But if consumers have bought both the car and the badge, they are free to do as they please with them.

WORLD MONUMENT TOURS

Mass tourism is doomed. Its carbon footprint alone means it is unsustainable. In the next twenty years, as political and economic pressures force the price of fuel upwards, it will become unaffordable in any event. There is an alternative, based on the saying "If Mohammed can't go to the mountain, let the mountain come to Mohammed."

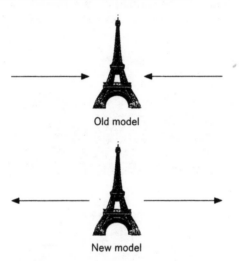

Old model

New model

With modern transportation technology, it would be perfectly possible to dismantle some of the world's main tourist attractions and take them on tour. The Eiffel Tower is an obvious candidate, but others spring to mind: the Statue of Liberty, Stonehenge, chunks of the Great Wall of China, and perhaps a couple of the smaller pyramids.

"World monument tours" would be much more ecologically friendly, and would generate huge revenues – after all, most people will be saving thousands by not travelling abroad to visit the monument, so they won't mind paying hundreds to see it at home.

NICOTINE SUPPLEMENT DEODORANT

Thanks to the smoking ban, the market for anti-smoking aids is more buoyant than ever. Current solutions such as nicotine patches and pills are far from perfect – you have to remember to take them. A nicotine-enhanced deodorant would deliver the nicotine fix straight to the blood vessels in the armpit, and wouldn't require consumers to change their everyday routine.

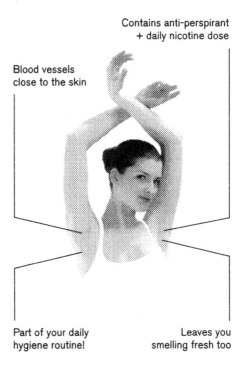

Contains anti-perspirant
+ daily nicotine dose

Blood vessels
close to the skin

Part of your daily
hygiene routine!

Leaves you
smelling fresh too

ELDER COACHING

"Life coaching" is now a billion-dollar industry. Such is the need for guidance that anyone can now set up as a coach, and find a keen audience for their expensive yet ill-informed advice. There is an ideal opportunity here for genuinely useful experience: that of our elders and betters.

Experience bringing up children, grandchildren, great-grandchildren

Decades of hard-earned wisdom

Personal knowledge of 85% of health problems

Several wars, with scars to prove it

Understanding of what truly matters in life

Reserves of useful sayings, proverbs, anecdotes

In most cultures, the elderly are revered for their knowledge and perspective. "Elder coaching" would take place in retirement homes, where groups of retirees would welcome clients and help them deal with their problems. For a mere £80 an hour, anyone can benefit from lifetimes of learning...

"MINI-PROSTITUTION" RING

There is a gap in the market between full-blown prostitution on one hand, and legitimate massage services on the other. As any hooker will tell you, many clients are not seeking to recreate a porn film; they just want a nice hug. "Mini-prostitution" would serve this niche. It would also attract many new customers, both male and female, who are currently put off by the sordidness of the profession. And whereas pimping is a criminal offence, providing companionship services that stop short of sex is quite legal, and potentially very lucrative.

£5	Kiss on the cheek (dry)
£8	Kiss on the cheek (wet)
£10	Ruffling of hair
£15	Five-minute hug
£20	Stroking of neck
£25	Patting of knee
£30	Pressing head against clothed bosom
£40	Nibbling of ear in private
£50	Nibbling of ear in public

IMMORTALITY PR

Immortality is due for a comeback. In centuries past, the wealthy would spend fortunes trying to ensure they were remembered after their death. That basic human urge has receded in our age of immediate gratification, but it is there to be revived. An "Immortality PR Agency" would promote people after their death. It would draft their obituary, publicize their lifetime achievements, and lobby publishers to include them in history textbooks.

Jane Trantmann
Housewife
(1948–2008)

"Created a radical new knitting stitch"

Mark Saville
Bank manager
(1937–2009)

"Famed for his ironic memos"

Jim Potts
Taxi driver
(1956–2008)

"Predicted the popularity of reality TV"

Customers would leave a pre-agreed budget to the agency in their will. £5,000 would guarantee their obituary was emailed to major news organizations worldwide. £50,000 would pay for a statue in a local park. £500,000 would buy a star-studded funeral. And £5,000,000 would pay for a 10-year public campaign to have their remains transferred to Westminster Abbey.

APPENDIX-FREEZING

The appendix is a much-maligned organ.
There is no clear scientific explanation
of its evolutionary function, yet most
physicians are happy for it to be discarded
under the pretext of inflammation. This is
short-sighted: for all we know, the appendix
could be beginning its evolutionary journey
– it might prove indispensable during
long-distance space travel, for example.
Cryopreservation of the appendix:

1.  After extraction, the appendix is cooled to extreme sub-zero temperatures (-196 °C)

2.  Cryoprotectant fluid is pumped into the appendix using a vitrification process

3. 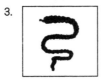 Now that the water in the appendix has been replaced by preservative chemicals, the appendix can be kept in storage until its owner needs it back

The science in this area is embryonic, but it
would seem prudent to preserve one's appendix
if possible, just in case one ever needs it again.

Basic procedure: $9,500 + $1,600 annual storage fee.

ANTI-ALLERGY PACK FOR KIDS

Today's children are developing asthma and other auto-immune-system diseases in greater numbers, because they are exposed to fewer germs than their parents' generation. An anti-allergy pack would contain samples of various kinds of dirt with which parents could discreetly infect their kids, so that they develop immunity.

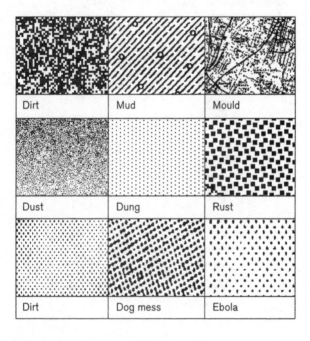

Dirt	Mud	Mould
Dust	Dung	Rust
Dirt	Dog mess	Ebola

Parents simply rub a pinch into a scratch or other open wound, and keep an eye out for any high fever that fails to abate within 48 hours.

PSYCHOTHERAPIST MATCHMAKING SERVICE

The long-term success of a couple is determined not by their initial sexual attraction, which fades over time, but by the compatibility of their underlying psychological types. Opposites attract but don't last: even though a naturally cautious woman may be swept away by her wild boyfriend to begin with, their fundamentally opposed profiles mean that their relationship is doomed. The average would-be lover is not in a position to judge such matters competently, which is why the divorce rate is so high. The solution? Let professional psychotherapists match up their clients, based on intimate knowledge of their deepest childhood-related psychoses. Example:

Peter Harlow
Narcissistic with egomaniac tendencies, due to insufficient parental love at age 2

+

Susie Kalbach
Dependent personality, submissive clinging behaviour, lack of self-confidence

Marriage approved:

Dr Grussman   Dr Frankzeiger

For a fee*, psychotherapists across the UK would consult their database of clients, and work out suitable pairings. The chosen couples would then marry, safe in the knowledge that their compatibility has been expertly determined.

* Suggested fee: £1,000/year for the duration of the relationship, with 50% back in case of divorce. £500 to the psychotherapist, £500 to the management agency.

PERSONAL ONLINE ADVERTISING

There are now over 100 million blogs worldwide. 120 million people have a MySpace profile. Over 65,000 videos are posted every day on YouTube. Millions of people are spending hours expressing themselves online and creating content, in the hope of some recognition or acknowlegement. Why not enable them to advertise?

A personal advertising site would allow them to translate their blogs, videos and rants into banner ads, which could then run across the internet for £5 or £10 a month, and draw viewers to their sites.

Business model: of the 200 million people with a social networking presence, aim for 1 million users paying £5 a month = £60 million turnover.

POISONED BILLS

UK companies waste a huge amount of time and money chasing late payments. Debt recovery could be accelerated by using an old-fashioned technique: the poisoned letter.

Account: 48645 00 7653 1
Our ref: 7896875-VH564/2/78

CentraFuels™

Dear Customer,

Our records indicate that you owe us the sum of: £126.87.

Please pay within 14 days. If you do not pay within 14 days, the poison in this letter will severely incapacitate or kill you. If you pay now by calling 0845 523 148, we will send you the antidote at no extra charge (allow 5 working days for delivery). If not, you may die.

CentraFuels looks forward to your continuing custom. If you have already paid, please ignore this letter.

Kind regards,

A. Collins

Head of Customer Relations

Paper soaked in odourless dioxins (concentration: 300pg-TEQ/g)

"LOOTING STORES"

As the events in New Orleans in 2006 reminded us, everyone loves to loot given half a chance. Looting taps into our primeval urges: faced with plenty, we are programmed to gorge ourselves, as there is no telling when we might be able to feast next. Looting also provides a deeply satisfying release from the constricted, penny-pinching, law-abiding persona that protestant capitalism imposes on us all. "Looting Stores" would stock the full range of consumer goods. Once a week, at a random time, a siren would sound and shoppers would be allowed to loot as much as they physically can in the following five minutes.

LOOTING RULES

1. You may only loot when the siren sounds. When the siren stops, you must stop looting immediately, or face prosecution. Any goods still inside the shop must be either paid for, or returned to their original position.

2. You may not use violence towards staff or other looters. Screaming, cheering, whooping and other general exuberance, however, are allowed.

3. There is a £1 entrance fee to the stores. This is to fund the looting and deter hangers-on. It is the small price you pay for the chance to participate in the looting.

4. You may not loot store fixtures, nor cash from the tills.

5. No pets.

THE "AVERSION DIET"

Most diets are far too complicated. Carbohydrate content, GI indexes and other macrobiotic nonsense only make it less likely that the diet will be followed. The "Aversion Diet" works on a very basic principle: if people eat less, they'll lose weight. All they need do is open the "Aversion Diet Handbook" (£19.99) and stare at its carefully-selected images during mealtimes. Guaranteed results within a month!

Fig. 1

Fig. 2   Fig. 3   Fig. 4

"Forget Atkins: simply read the Aversion Diet Handbook at mealtimes, and lose your appetite pronto. The "Aversion Diet": available on DVD, on mobiles, in one-to-one sessions, in hypnosis format. For those who've tried everything."

TAGGED "SEXUAL FANTASIES" WEBSITE

Erotic fantasies about friends, neighbours and colleagues are universal, harmless and usually kept secret. Yet who wouldn't be curious about one's role in the sexual imaginings of another? A "tagged sexual fantasies site" would allow people to describe their fantasies and tag them with the real names of the people involved.

Anyone who logged on could discover how many fantasies there were involving them, pay £10 to read each one, and £50 to discover the identity of the fantasist.* The site would satisfy people's natural curiosity, help them understand how they are sexually perceived by others, and occasionally even open the door for the real thing.

* As long as the latter had originally agreed to have this divulged.

GUILT TRIP HOLIDAYS

No matter how unhappy or stressed you feel, there are others who are objectively much worse off. A "Guilt Trip!" tour operator would take disgruntled Westerners on holiday to some of the world's least privileged spots, so that they may learn to appreciate their relative good fortune and count their blessings. Possible destinations:

Swaziland
Life expectancy: 33
2 weeks touring
AIDS clinics: £1,999

Northern Sumatra
300,000 homeless
£1,599 (Stay with tsunami victims)

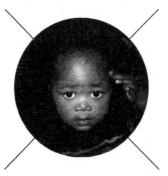

North Korea
Political prisoners: 200,000 (est.)
State-hosted guided tour: £2,400

Eritrea
Calories per day: <1500
£1,299 (Includes refugee camp visit)

SPONSORED VOICEMAIL ANSWERING MESSAGES

If mobile-phone users could get money off their bills, many of them would consent to their computerized voicemail message being subtly sponsored:

"Hello. The person you are trying to call is not available, possibly because they've gone to see that great new film that everyone's talking about, "Karate Bride", out now. Please leave a message after the beep."

"Hello. There is no one available to answer your call. That's because everyone's at the Couch Superstore Easter Bargain 70% Off supersale! Hurry Hurry! Or leave a message."

"It has not been possible to reach your correspondent at this time. Please try again later. Or switch on to Channel 17 right this very minute to watch 'America's Fattest Models'!"

Advertiser pays 10p per message.
Consumer gets 5p off phone bill.
Profit for you: 5p per message!

PERSONAL BLACK BOX

Flying may be the safest form of travel, but still, accidents do happen, and when they do, passengers are often aware of their impending fate for minutes on end, as their craft plummets to the ground.

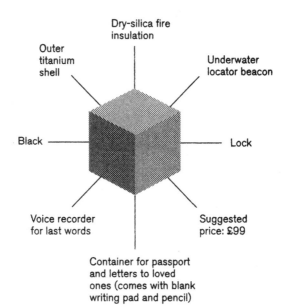

Dry-silica fire insulation

Outer titanium shell

Underwater locator beacon

Black

Lock

Voice recorder for last words

Suggested price: £99

Container for passport and letters to loved ones (comes with blank writing pad and pencil)

The "personal black box" would ensure that a passenger's last message to his loved ones survived the crash. Like a normal black box, it would be built to resist fire, salt water and the force of the impact. Rescue teams would collect it thanks to its beacon and deliver it to the family, affording them some crumb of comfort in their grief.

For sale in airports. Or free when you've collected 5,000 air miles!

SOUNDPROOF PRIMAL-SCREAM BOOTHS

Primal-screaming is a well-established therapeutical method, with immediate benefits in stress reduction, anger management and general cardiovascular fitness. The only obstacle to its widespread use is the lack of appropriate facilities: primal-screaming in the modern-day open-plan office is impractical. Soundproof booths in busy city locations would solve the problem.

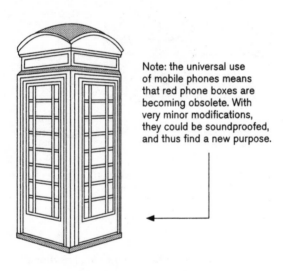

Note: the universal use of mobile phones means that red phone boxes are becoming obsolete. With very minor modifications, they could be soundproofed, and thus find a new purpose.

Stressed office workers, shoppers and commuters would pay £1 for 2 minutes of unrestrained primal screaming, and emerge from the booth with their equanimity restored.

RELATIONSHIP HEADHUNTERS

In the recruitment industry, there is a basic difference between headhunters and mere recruiters. Recruiters wait for candidates to apply to them – which often means they get people who have been fired, made redundant, or who simply weren't successful in their career. Headhunters, on the other hand, actively pursue the best candidates, even if they already have a great job – and the best usually do. This is why headhunting agencies can charge a lot more than recruitment agencies. The same logic could be applied to relationships: all the most attractive people are usually taken.

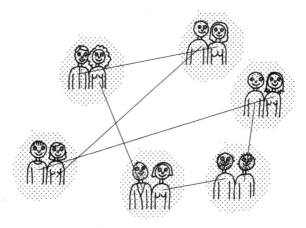

"Relationship headhunters" would not just restrict themselves to single available prospects, but would actively try to convince people to ditch their current partner in favour of the headhunter's much more eligible client. After all, why miss out on the love of your life simply because they're with someone else?

DICTATOR MAKEOVER SERVICE

Whether we like it or not, our world is driven by image and spin. Much of the current crisis with North Korea, for instance, is due to perceptions of Kim Jong-Il as a madman. Western media reinforce this by focusing on his Elvis hairdo, his suits, his lifestyle. It would therefore be in Kim's interest to undergo a relatively painless image makeover so as to end North Korea's international isolation and defuse global military tension. Other leaders with deranged reputations, such as Iran's Mahmoud Ahmadinejad, would also benefit.

Before

After

MAKEOVER BUDGET

Flight to London (return, via Bangkok)	£1,550
Selfridges personal shopper budget	£5,000
Haircut and male grooming	£90
Anger-management counselling	£120
Hotel (two nights)	£320
Expenses	£100
Makeover fee	*£1,000*
Total	£8,180

Offer to help by sending your makeover proposals to: Kim Jong-Il, Standing Committee, Supreme People's Assembly, Pyongyang 34, North Korea.

POSITIVE PREGNANCY TEST

The problem: In this age of commitment-phobic men, the modern woman needs to determine if her boyfriend is serious about her, or if she's wasting her precious time. The solution: A pregnancy kit that enables women to fake pregnancy – the only kit on the market that always reacts positive!

CONSUMER INSTRUCTIONS

1) Hold the absorbent tip in urine stream. In under one minute, the "yes" window will turn blue.
2) Show positive result to boyfriend, remembering to act surprised.
3) Gauge his reaction. If he storms out, wails, gnashes his teeth or some combination thereof, he is not serious about you and you should terminate the relationship.
4) If he hugs you and cries tears of joy, he is serious and you should come clean about your little subterfuge as gently as possible.
   Then get pregnant for real.

£9.99. To be sold in all good pharmacies. Available without medical prescription.

CELEBRITY-ZAPPING
TV CHANNEL

Launch a TV channel that relays whatever
is playing on a celebrity's home TV set, so
that fans can watch whatever their star
happens to be watching. Participating stars
would gain fan loyalty and 50% of the profits.

Pre-agreed royalties would be paid to whatever
channels the star watched. And revenue would
come from advertising and subscriptions.

ASTROLOGICAL LOTTERY

People who play the lottery usually also believe
in horoscopes. Yet no one has thought to
make these two superstitions work together
systematically. The principle is simple: if someone
normally plays £1 on the lottery every week,
they just hand over their £52 for the year, and
the "Astrological Lottery" would play it all on
the few weeks when their horoscope is favourable,
thus maximising their probability of a win.

The market:

People
who play the
lottery

People who
believe in
astrology

Non-superstitious people

Example: Elin D. is a Virgo, with Aries Ascendant.
The moon will slope into her orbit from 21 June
through September, during which time her stars
will be aligned. Venus will also be propitious
from mid-January to late February. Her £52
will be invested in astrological lottery tickets
during those lucky weeks. In November, however,
she comes under the rule of Pluto, the planet of
death. No point playing then, Elin D.!

THE "PIGGY BANK" BANK

Start a bank aimed at children. Childhood is the perfect time to save for retirement. Firstly, the maths of compound interest means that the money will go a lot further: £5 saved at the age of 6 will be worth more by retirement age than £100 saved at the age of 30. Secondly, kids don't care about money in itself, they just care about fun. The "Piggy Bank" Bank's branches would be shaped like huge pink piggy banks, turning the chore of saving into a magical experience.

Drop your pocket money into the piggy's automated slot!

"Fun" interest rates, like 3.33% or 1.23456789%!

Staff dressed in piggy costumes

Manager oinks!

ALTERNATIVE SPORTS COMMENTARY

With the technology available these days, there is no reason why sports fans should be restricted to the official mainstream commentary of any match or event. The same visuals could be accompanied by a choice of commentaries, to cater for a much wider variety of audience niches, including for instance:

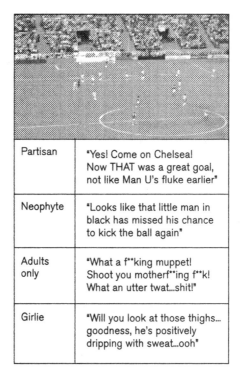

Partisan	"Yes! Come on Chelsea! Now THAT was a great goal, not like Man U's fluke earlier"
Neophyte	"Looks like that little man in black has missed his chance to kick the ball again"
Adults only	"What a f**king muppet! Shoot you motherf**ing f**k! What an utter twat...shit!"
Girlie	"Will you look at those thighs... goodness, he's positively dripping with sweat...ooh"

SELF-ACUPUNCTURE KIT

The problem: Acupuncture constitutes a proven cure for many ills, as well as a great all-round relaxant. However, undergoing regular treatment at the hands of a trained expert is expensive and inconvenient.

The science: New research* shows that it doesn't really matter where you stick the acupuncture needles; it's the fact of pricking yourself at all that rouses various hormones and improves your blood flow, thus benefiting your health and well-being.

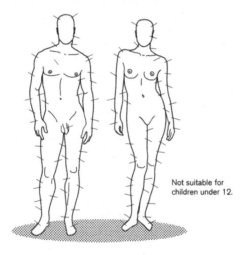

Not suitable for children under 12.

The solution: A "self-acupuncture" kit would allow millions to try the venerable art of acupuncture in the safety of their own home.

Contains: 50 dishwasher-friendly needles, a diagram of the human body and "how to get started" instructions. Suggested price: £25.99.
* 'Acupuncture for patients with migraine: a randomized controlled trial' (Linde et al, Journal of American Medical Association, 2005)

BIBLE OF BIBLES

God presents himself to us in many different guises, through many different religions, each with their own sacred text. It would be hugely practical to combine these into one handy volume, so that all of his (or her!) wisdom and instructions can be more easily consulted. Includes:

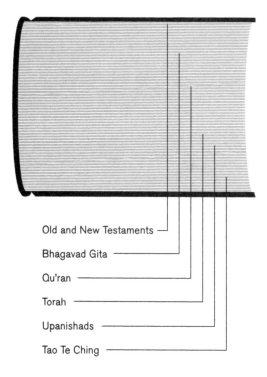

Old and New Testaments

Bhagavad Gita

Qu'ran

Torah

Upanishads

Tao Te Ching

The Bible of Bibles. If there is a God, he's in here! £19.99 only!

"HERMIT BROTHER" TV SHOW

The most popular bit of *Big Brother* is the diary room, where contestants are on their own. Why not take this further and feature only one contestant, whom we would get to know intimately over 2 or 3 months?

Hermit Brother! Coming Soon!

- Expert hermits give advice and comment
- No prize money needed
- No risk of violence/sex/racism involving other contestants
- Evict him (or her) at the end anyway

NB: Important to cast someone interesting

"TIME IS MONEY" PHONE DOWNLOAD

For the demotivated employee: a mobile download that beeps encouragingly every time they've earned £1.

How it would work:

1) Demotivated employee downloads software to their mobile (£5 charge)

2) Demotivated employee inputs annual income

3) Demotivated employee's mobile beeps every time they earn £1

4) Motivation increases!

Examples (based on an 8-hour-day, 240 days a year):

Name:	Occupation:	Annual income:	Phone beeps every:
John P.	City trader	£2,000,000	3.5 secs
Sally M.	Ad exec	£150,000	46 secs
David E.	IT	£61,000	1 min 53 secs
Paula W.	Teacher	£32,000	3 min 36 secs
Bob	Shelf stacker	£9,500	12 min 7 secs

MICRO-MORTGAGES

There is no reason why the essential
consumer benefit of mortgages, which is
the ability to spread payments into
manageable amounts over the course of a
lifetime, could not be extended to smaller
items. As long as someone's credit rating
allowed it, why not let them pay for a
sandwich or a CD over 25 years or longer?

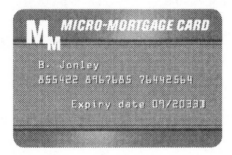

Item	Price	Monthly payment for the next 25 years including interest
Flowers	£6	4p
Magazine	£3.10	2p
Bottle of wine	£12	8p
Cinema ticket	£7.50	5p
Meal for two	£68	45p
Haircut	£35	23p

SHOWER KARAOKE

Millions of music-lovers worldwide begin the day with a singsong in the shower. Enhance their artistic pleasure with the "shower karaoke", a waterproof, fix-to-the-wall device that comes with the lyrics of thousands of songs in karaoke format. Interactive version: Once you have established the "shower karaoke" market, move it to the next level by going interactive. Each "shower karaoke" could be linked to the owner's internet connection wirelessly, enabling him or her to sing along live with others around the globe.

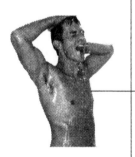

Karaoke shower choir no 548/a:
La Traviata (Verdi)
Every morning 7.30 to 7.40 GMT
(currently on Act II Scene 6).
Royalties to join in: £0.50/day

Karaoke shower choir no 28/f:
Ring Cycle (Wagner)
Weekdays 6 a.m. Pacific Standard Time
(currently Götterdämmerung Act I
Scene 5 Parsifal Aria).
Royalties to join in: $1.05/day

Karaoke shower choir no 6601/b:
Gilbert & Sullivan
"The Paid Piper" Act II "Blimey"
Weekends 10–10.30 a.m.
Royalties to join in: £0.80/day

ONLINE MIRROR

Wives and girlfriends usually turn to their partner before going out to check that they look good. Single women (and single fashion-conscious guys) don't have that option. One solution would be to create a mirror with an integrated camera that is linked to the net. Ladies would turn it on when they want immediate fashion feedback from online experts.

Sample expert feedback
"Love the hat!"
"Blue is so not your colour!"
"Looking good honey"
"Those boots are so now!"

£1/minute

STRANGER BUSINESS CARDS

We are surrounded by strangers in our daily lives, but rarely have the opportunity to interact with them; "stranger business cards" would provide an easy and non-threatening way of making contact. Simply hand over the relevant card to a stranger without saying a word – should they be interested in meeting you, they now have your details.

You look nice.
Get in touch
sometime!

I loved the book you're
reading. Call me when
you've finished it and
let me know what you
thought!

If you ever break
up with your partner,
here's my number.

I don't know you
but I wish you
well in your life.

Smile!
It might never happen.

I commute on
this tube line too.
Next time, let's talk!

Suggested price: £9.99 for a pack of 100

RENT-A-MUSE

Our modern knowledge economy runs on constant innovation. Never has there been such a widespread need for new ideas. The muse is the traditional source of creative inspiration, a conduit from the Gods to us mere mortals. A rent-a-muse agency would find and hire out particularly inspiring individuals, whose mere presence sparks novel thoughts.

Muse: Lavinia

Inspires traditional
artistic and literary ideas

£120/hour

Muse: Roxana

Great at inspiring advertising
and marketing ideas

£240/hour

Muse: Talulla

Best for business and
corporate acquisition ideas

£500/hour

Muse: Barry

Inspires home
redecoration ideas

£25/hour

FREELANCE PARKING ATTENDANTS

Start a scheme whereby anyone who texts the location of an illegally-parked car to the traffic warden firm gets 10% of the fine. With the best will in the world, traffic warden firms can't cover the whole country, and therefore miss out on thousands of potential fines a day. With this scheme, they could employ millions of citizens to assist them in enforcing the law – and turning a profit!

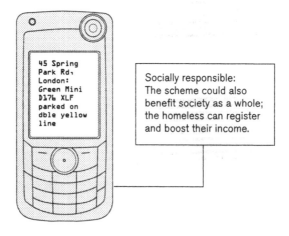

45 Spring
Park Rd,
London:
Green Mini
D176 XLF
parked on
dble yellow
line

Socially responsible:
The scheme could also benefit society as a whole; the homeless can register and boost their income.

Members of the public would discreetly text the details of the parking offence to NCP or similar parking fine firms. These partner firms would then direct one of their full-time traffic wardens to the scene to confirm the sighting and impose a fine. Given an average fine of £80, the freelance traffic wardens could make £8 for a mere ten seconds' work.

CONTROLLED DRUG-TAKING CLINICS

Future civilization will look back on our society's demonization of drugs with amused curiosity. Why on earth should mankind not experiment with mind-altering substances, if they are available? Like Aldous Huxley, who wrote *The Doors Of Perception* to relate his experiments with mescalin, there are many well-adjusted, upstanding members of society who would love to try heroin or LSD just once, to observe their effects and explore the limits of consciousness.

This could be done under medical supervision, in a comfortable and safe environment, and in a country where the laws are not so small-minded. Under these conditions, thousands would flock to these clinics for a new experience, without fear of public censure, or of turning into junkies.

ANTI-JEHOVAH'S WITNESS LITERATURE

Most people will have received a knock on the door from Jehovah's Witnesses at some point, and will know they are well-meaning but extremely persistent. Now householders can turn the tables on them with the "Anti-Jehovah's Witness kit"! When they come knocking, explain that you are busy right now, but would love to chat to them when they have read your literature. Simply hand them the four-volume kit, and close the door.

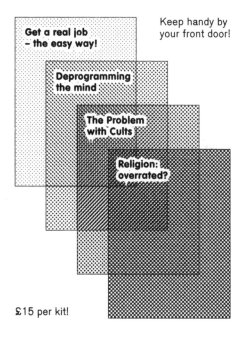

Get a real job
– the easy way!

Keep handy by
your front door!

Deprogramming
the mind

The Problem
with Cults

Religion:
overrated?

£15 per kit!

CONVINCE THE CHINESE TO SWITCH TO KNIVES AND FORKS

Since 1980, protein consumption in China has quadrupled. Economic growth has seen a huge increase in demand for meat that shows no sign of abating. This could provide the catalyst for an even more dramatic shift: a campaign to convince the 1.3 billion Chinese to abandon chopsticks in favour of the more meat-friendly Western knife and fork. This would require a culturally sensitive advertising push, illustrating the benefits of the knife and fork, and indeed making their use aspirational, a sign of middle-class success.

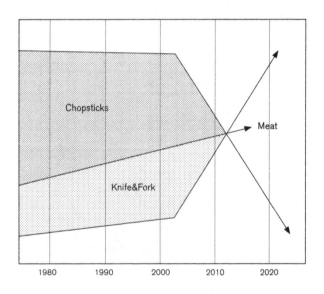

The prize would be huge: Even assuming a small profit margin of 10p per knife and fork, and assuming – frugally – one set per inhabitant per year, annual profits would total £100 million.

RUNOVERBYABUS.COM

The service: register at runoverbyabus.com and draft those final emails to your family and friends, telling them how much you really loved them.

The problem: every year, thousands of people die in tragic unexpected accidents, without being able to say goodbye to their nearest and dearest.

The idea: a website where you can write emails that will be sent to loved ones should you die suddenly.

The opportunity: set up a direct debit of say £1 a month. Should you die suddenly, your bank account will be cancelled, the direct debits will cease, and the emails will be sent off automatically.

The benefit: for a tiny sum, you can go about your daily business secure in the knowledge that your final goodbyes will be taken care of.

EXTREME T-SHIRTS

Fashion and reality collide in this exclusive
limited T-shirt brand: 10% of the price of each
T-shirt goes towards a spectacular real-life
event that could await you if you wear it.

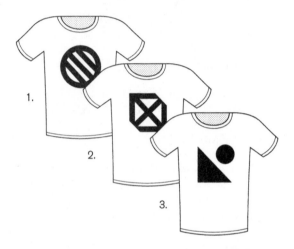

1. A stunning high-class international escort
has been paid £5,000 to seduce any wearer of
this T-shirt and give him the night of his life.*

2. A bank branch somewhere in the world has
been instructed to deliver £100,000 cash to
the first wearer of this T-shirt to walk through
its doors.

3. A trained ex-KGB assassin has been paid
£10,000 to kneecap anyone wearing this
T-shirt on sight.

* Female, gay and lesbian versions available

ELECTRONIC SWEARBOX

Voice-recognition technology is now so advanced
that it can pick out not just individual words in
conversation, but also recognize who uttered them.
It has become entirely feasible to create a piece of
software that would run on a family or office computer,
pick up specified swear words, and penalize the offender
by debiting their credit card or paycheque directly.

```
JOHNSON FAMILY

          DATE        SWEAR WORD    AMOUNT

DAD       03/02/08    BUGGER        30P
          10/02/08    WANKERS       £1
          11/02/08    F**KING       £2
          11/02/08    HELL          50P
          11/02/08    BITCH         £1
          11/02/08    F**K (OFF)    £2
          15/02/08    BUGGER        30P
          16/02/08    CRETINS       20P
          22/02/08    GODDAMN       20P
          23/02/08    BLOODY        20P
          27/02/08    BUGGER        30P
          TOtal:                    £8

MUM       01/02/08    DAMN          15P
          11/02/08    PISSED        20P
          11/02/08    BASTARD       50P
          11/02/08    F**K (OFF)    £2
          11/02/08    WANKER        £1
          11/02/08    ARSEHOLE      £1
          16/02/08    BLOODY        20P
          23/02/08    DAMN          15P
          TOtal:                    £5.20

FREDDY    02/02/08    RETARD        £1.50
          03/02/08    GAY           £2
          11/02/08    F**KWITS      £1.20
          12/02/08    F**KWITS      £1.20
          14/02/08    RETARD        £1.50
          19/02/08    RETARD        £1.50
          19/02/08    F**KWIT       £1.20
          21/02/08    F**KWAD       £1.30
          TOtal:                    £11.40

LIZZIE    27/02/08    BURP!         10P
          TOtal:                    10P
```

The offender would receive an invoice every month
detailing the swearing, and giving them information
as to their swearing trends.

ONLINE FIREWORKS

Everyone loves fireworks. But they are difficult to organize and require time-consuming safety precautions – not to mention local authority approval. A computerized fireworks range built in an uninhabited area like the Sahara desert would allow people to programme and set off their own fireworks display, and watch it live online.

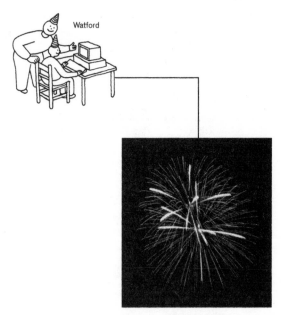

Watford

Moroccan desert

Basic £100 package includes: 3 Palm Multi-break shells, 4 Chrysanthemum shells (24 shots), 6 Meteor Showers, 2 Ring Shells (choice of colours), 20 Stars, 1 Thunder Storm Serpentine Multi-break Shell, 10 Single-burst Fireballs.

"PAUPER MONTHLY" MAGAZINE

Research shows that happiness is relative, particularly when it comes to money. How much you earn in absolute terms does not affect your happiness levels (beyond a certain minimum). What makes a difference is how much you earn relative to your peers. As the media exposes us to a diet of celebrities, huge City bonuses and aspirational advertising, it is no surprise we are unhappy – we end up overestimating how rich other people are.

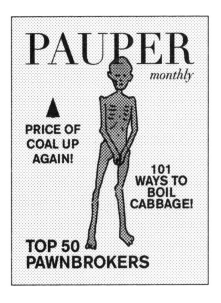

"Pauper Monthly" would counteract this trend; by showcasing the life of the poor, it would make most of us feel luckier, and therefore happier. Not only that, but 10% of the cover price could go to charity, thereby improving the lot of the truly poor as well.

CASHPOINT LOTTERY

More and more banks are threatening to impose charges for providing cashpoints. Yet there is a simple and profitable solution: a cashpoint lottery, where punters can stick their card in, play £5 on the slot/cash machine lottery and win the jackpot!*

Cashpoints:
Boring
Predictable
"Everyday"

+

Gambling:
Elitist
Casino-based
"Special occasion"

=

CASHPOINT LOTTERY!

Transforms entering your PIN from a chore into a life-changing experience!

* For every £5 played, every 50th person wins £100.

REAL VIRAL ADVERTISING

Genetically engineer a highly contagious real virus that makes a brand's logo appear on people's skin. Once the basic formula has been cracked, simply change the shape and colour to suit different advertisers.

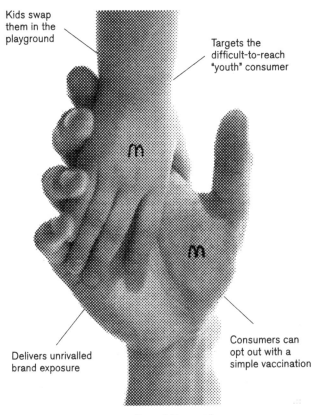

Kids swap them in the playground

Targets the difficult-to-reach "youth" consumer

Delivers unrivalled brand exposure

Consumers can opt out with a simple vaccination

Also available as a rash

ANGER MANAGEMENT WARS

Recent research suggests that wars are caused not by political reasons, or by shortages of resources, but simply by the number of young men in any given society – as the authors of one report put it, "countries with relatively large numbers of young males are more likely to experience episodes of coalitional aggression."*

War	War 1	War 2	War 3
Dates	19 July 2009	31 October 2010	29 December 2008
Location	Namibian desert	Australian Outback	Siberia
Numbers expected	20,000	105,000	4,500
Level of anger	****	***	****** (nuclear)
Prize for survivors	Playstation	Free holiday	Brand new 4x4

For an affordable sum (£500), and with weapons subsidized by the taxpayer, angry young men from all countries would be encouraged to join in an organized war in some remote location, perhaps with a prize for those still alive at the end. It would only formalize the age-old process, but would suit both society at large and these aggressive young men – leaving the rest of us out of it and producing a healthy profit for the organizers.

* Mesquida and Wiener, 2001, York University

FAKE WINDOWS FOR PLANES

Fear of flying affects up to 40% of passengers, with some people too scared to fly at all. Airlines would welcome a cheap but effective solution to prevent the lost business. "Fake window views" are high-quality cardboard inserts, designed to fit the window shapes on the most common planes used by the airline industry*.

"Fake window views" range:

1.
2.
3.

1. "In a car on the motorway"
2. "In a train passing a green field"
3. "Windsurfing within yards of the beach"

"Fake window views" fool the passenger's brain into believing that they're not flying at all, but are engaged in some other form of familiar, reassuring motion. There are 3.5 billion seats sold every year**. If we assume 40% of those are blighted by fear of flying, that represents a market of 1.4 billion. Each "Fake window view" should cost no more than 50p to the airline, yielding a potential annual turnover of £700 million. Going forward, the technology could be adapted to the – much scarier – experience of space travel.

* Airbus 350, Boeing 787, Boeing 767, Airbus 340, Airbus 320, Boeing 757, Boeing 747, Boeing 737 **Official Airline Guide Report 2007

POST-APOCALYPSE INSURANCE

There is a gap in the insurance market, as anyone who has read the small print will know; most policies are null and void in case of nuclear war, major disaster, or anything drastic enough to merit the title "act of God". Yet this surely is when insurance is most needed. For a fairly steep premium, post-apocalypse insurers would guarantee to come and rescue clients in the aftermath of a nuclear conflict, or other catastrophic event.

£5,562/year

"Peace of mind in time of war"

Policy details:
– GPS tracker implanted under your skin
– Free rescue service by a SWAT team within 48 hours
– Medical care for radiation burns
– Your own ensuite room in a luxury nuclear bunker
– Priority seat in any evacuation to another planet

RELATIONSHIP LOYALTY CARDS

The early stages of a relationship are a minefield of misunderstandings, hormonal confusion and uncertain etiquette. At what point does a fling turn into something more enduring? A "relationship loyalty card" would provide clear ethical guidelines. It allows lovebirds 10 casual sex encounters before things are deemed to have become serious. On the first date, the couple fill in the card. It is then the gentleman's responsibility to punch it after every sexual session, until the tenth, when the couple are automatically declared to be "together", thus avoiding the usual awkwardness.

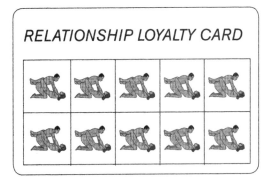

Business model: the card could be sponsored by a suitable brand e.g. a condom manufacturer, or you could even charge people for its use, with free arbitration thrown in and a money-back guarantee if the relationship fails.

SECOND INTERNET

The internet is nearing breaking point. Spam is ubiquitous. Cybercrime is rife. Pornography is rampant. Google is all-powerful. It is time for a second, parallel internet. The second internet would charge a fee for access, and so provide a far more streamlined and exclusive arena, free of the garbage that clutters the original. It would still use the physical cables, routers and other current infrastructure, but would only be accessible to subscribers.

Technical practicalities

a) It would be too expensive initially to replace the actual physical backbone of the net.

b) Instead, one would set up a number of DNS servers that would act as root servers for a new root domain which only exists in that DNS name-space. Effectively it would be a private DNS network.

c) Users would download a piece of software that reconfigures their computer's TCP/IP, following the simple instructions for their computer platform.

d) They could then access a whole world of new websites that the old internet DNS servers wouldn't be able to recognize.

Entirely new websites would be created there, with new forms of e-commerce, advertising, social networking and so on, all under the supervision of a benevolent authority. Like the early American Pilgrims, the early second internet adopters would face great challenges, but would eventually forge a better internet than the corrupt one they'd left behind.

BEGINNERS' GYMS

Gyms can be very intimidating, particularly to new members, who don't yet know their way around the equipment – and who in any case may be a little overweight and self-conscious. A chain of beginners' gyms would boost recruitment amongst those who are too scared to join a proper gym. The equipment would be especially tailored to their lack of experience and fitness.

Fake weights: twice as light as advertised

Swimming pool full of salt water

Electrically-powered exercise bikes

Convex mirrors in changing rooms

After a year or so of beginners' exercise, and once they had learned the ropes, they would be able to progress to a normal gym without fear of ridicule.

EMBASSY-HOSTED PARTIES

Embassies are exempt from the jurisdiction of the host territory. Traditionally, this special status has only been abused for reasons of state, such as spying, but there is no reason why a poor nation might not seek to make money from it.

Burundi, for instance, with a GDP per capita of $700, could help fund itself by agreeing to host parties in its embassies worldwide, where all manner of drugs and debauchery could be provided without worrying about the local police barging in.

Guests would pay thousands for the privilege of breaking the law in such safe yet well-appointed settings. The country would receive much-needed foreign currency, and the organizers would take an appropriate cut.

SANTA LOST LIMB

Business case: Parents these days have a tough time convincing their cynical kids that Father Christmas exists. This original product answers that need: parents just stick it in the chimney on Christmas Day as proof that Santa came by. Market: The millions of parents who want to keep the magic of Christmas alive for their children.

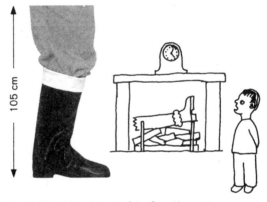

105 cm

- No visible blood (suitable for all ages)
- Reindeer fur for extra verisimilitude
- Wedge in chimney on Christmas morning
- Suggested retail price: £29.99.

For cheap and reliable manufacturing, try the Zhuhai Special Economic Zone, 11–15, North Haizhu Road, Yuexiu District, Guangzhou 510040, China.

DIVORCE FRIDGE MAGNETS

Divorcing couples often have to live under the same roof during proceedings, yet are usually keen to avoid each other as much as possible. A set of divorce fridge magnets would make the whole process easier to manage.

I'M
LEAVING YOU

I HATE
YOU !

YOU RUINED
MY LIFE

GOOD RIDDANCE

I'M TAKING THE
KIDS

CALL MY
LAWYER

I'M SLEEPING
ON THE COUCH

MY MOTHER
WARNED ME
ABOUT YOU

YOU CHEATING
BASTARD

I'LL SETTLE
FOR
THE HOUSE
THE CAT
£100,000
£500,000
£1,000,000

YOU CHEATING
SLUT

LAST MOMENTS INSURANCE

Make sure you die with as much dignity as you lived. Mozart is an oft-cited example: crippled by poverty and illness, the once-successful composer was buried in a pauper's grave...

"Last moments insurance" would guarantee that no matter how low you sank, your final hours would be dignified: for a mere £5 a month for most of your life, you would be entitled to a delicious last meal, your favourite film, satin sheets and even personalized suggestions as to memorable last words.*

* Requires written medical confirmation that you have less than 24 hours to live

"SURPRISE" BRAND

Everyone loves a surprise – yet they are usually reserved for birthdays and Christmas. A "Surprise" brand would sell a whole range of products, chosen for their quality and originality, but packaged to conceal their exact identity.

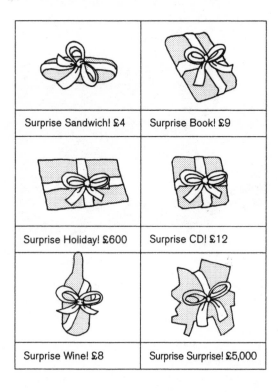

Surprise Sandwich! £4	Surprise Book! £9
Surprise Holiday! £600	Surprise CD! £12
Surprise Wine! £8	Surprise Surprise! £5,000

The consumer would pay a premium for the excitement of not knowing exactly what they're getting. The "surprises" would go on sale at all major retailers, and inject a little welcome unpredictability into the shopping experience.

YOUR COMPLETE WORKS

Who hasn't glanced with awe at the thick-bound volumes of a famous writer's complete works? Yet most people produce a similarly prodigious output over their lifetime, simply in the course of their day-to-day life and job. It may not make as compelling reading, but it's still worth preserving to its author. He or she would download simple keystroke-logging software that sends everything they type to a secure website. Every year, the result would be printed in a beautifully-bound volume, which can then take pride of place in the author's library.

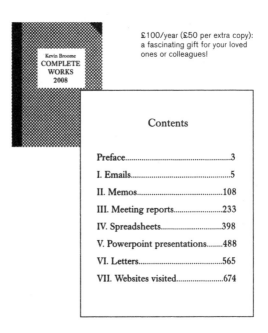

Kevin Broome
**COMPLETE WORKS
2008**

£100/year (£50 per extra copy): a fascinating gift for your loved ones or colleagues!

Contents

MULTI-ANGLE HAIRDRESSING

Multi-angle hairdressing would solve a fundamental problem: the client only gets to see the full haircut at the very end, when it's too late to remedy any misunderstandings. Several small digital cameras linked to a screen enable the client to switch between views of the haircut-in-progress, and nip any mistakes in the bud.

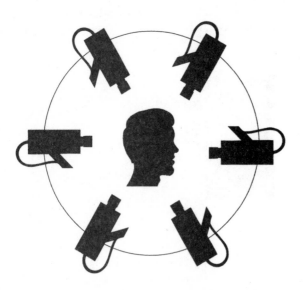

For a small upfront investment (£200/chair), the salon can thus guarantee satisfied customers, and prevent expensive lawsuits.

RELIGIOUS TWITTER

Twitter, for those who don't know, is a website that allows you to tell your friends what you're doing throughout the day, in very short messages, e.g.: "Just walking the dog", "Having a cup of tea" or "Daydreaming about Brad Pitt". This is entirely futile for most people, but a modified version could prove highly useful: a religious Twitter, where Catholics could post their sinful thoughts as soon as they occur, in a sort of permanent confession. Sample day:

9.15	"I'm lusting after a fellow commutress"
10.30	"I didn't leave the waitress a tip"
11.04	"I envied my colleague's new car"
13.17	"I just lied on my tax return"
13.25	"I'm drinking a third pint – and it's a weekday"
15.01	"I'm having doubts about transubstantiation"
16.52	"I'm being slothful at work"
16.53	"I am connecting to a sinful internet site"
16.54	"My loins are on fire"
17.01	"I have grievously sinned in the company bathroom"
19.12	"I lied to my wife about enjoying her cooking"
21.45	"I watched a revealing bra advert"
23.46	"I'm angry at my baby for crying"
23.59	"I let my wife get up to comfort it"

Posting a sin via SMS would cost 50p, thus providing immediate penance, as well as profit for the operator.

PRIVATE ALPHABET

It is becoming increasingly difficult for parents to find an original name for their newborn. Whereas twenty years ago, people were content with "Dave", "Pete" or "Sarah", now every child is called something quirky, so that "Scarletts", "Zanders" and other "Dakotas" have become commonplace. We have quite simply run out of names. What is required is a new alphabet entirely.

Twelve brand new letters such as the ones above would create millions of potential new names overnight. To cover the cost of introducing them to the world, their use would need to be licensed for a one-off lifetime £5 fee, which the parents would pay at birth (use of special typefaces is paid for on a similar licensed basis).

Example:

Brandμe

Pronounce: [Brand-yiee]

Thinking ahead: corporations could pay to use them too in naming their new products, for a higher fee of course.

JUDGEMENT DAY INTERVIEW TRAINING

Judgement Day awaits us all, yet how many of us prepare for it? It is literally the interview of your life, so it makes sense to rehearse – particularly when bungling it can have such long-term consequences. Potential market: The entire Christian world population, with particular focus on the affluent evangelical US sector. How to set up your very own "Judgement Day Interview Training" centre:

Features to include:

Interpreting God's body language

What to say to St Peter

When to argue, when to shut up

Hurry hurry! Don't wait till it's too late!

101 Tips from near-death experiences

Taught by bona fide defrocked priests

Suggested charges: £799 for basic module, £99 supplement for heavy sinners, £1,999 combined with last rites

PAY-YOUR-WAY HOSPITALS

Healthcare costs are spiralling, which means that the majority of patients are increasingly unable to afford the most effective treatment. The solution? A chain of private hospitals where patients may pay for treatment by working in bed as they recover.

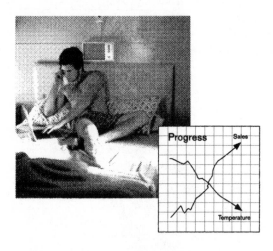

Most illnesses are only partly incapacitating, and leave the patient perfectly able to handle light tasks such as call-centre work, proofreading or knitting clothes – depending on their skillset. As they recover, their work helps pay for their operation and medication (as well as industry-standard management fees). Not only that, but the scheme may yield health benefits: medical practitioners agree that activity shortens recovery times for a wide range of ailments. As the saying goes, hard work never killed anyone – unlike, say, cancer.

SUBSTITUTE PROTESTERS

Many of us wish we could have our say on the streets by demonstrating, but we simply don't have the time. "Substitute protesters" could march on our behalf, for a small fee. The service could also include a personalized message, which the protester would wave about for you. Proposed tariffs below.

One-hour peaceful march	£20
One-hour sit-in	£17.50
Two-hour march	£35
Holding placard	£5
Waving placard	£15
Bashing police with placard	£75
Night in cells	£250
Ten marches per year bundle	£300

BIOLOGICAL CLOCK

According to the media, women are reputedly obsessed with their "biological clock", yet there are none even on the market. A digital countdown clock would provide women with a clear reminder of how many years, months, days, minutes and seconds they have left to conceive.

"Biological watch" portable version
Alarm rings once a week when you reach 30, gradually louder

Luxury mantelpiece version
Reset it and pass it on to your daughter when she reaches 18!

Women would input their date of birth, and the quartz-mechanism clock would automatically count down to the moment they reach 36, the medically-recommended latest age for procreation. Market: fertile women (18-35) wishing to raise a family (estimate: 309,000,000 million worldwide).

"SEX DRUGS AND ROCK'N'ROLL" STORES

The idea is to start a chain of lifestyle stores based on the famous concept of "sex drugs and rock'n'roll". No one has yet thought to combine these three highly complementary businesses into one. Each store to comprise:

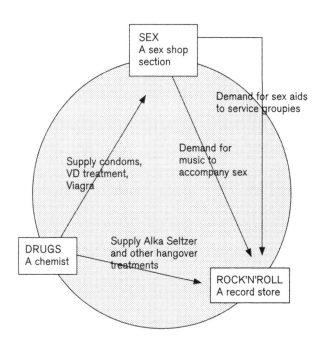

SEX
A sex shop section

Demand for sex aids to service groupies

Supply condoms, VD treatment, Viagra

Demand for music to accompany sex

Supply Alka Seltzer and other hangover treatments

DRUGS
A chemist

ROCK'N'ROLL
A record store

PRE-WORK RETIREMENT

Retirement is wasted on the elderly. Some people would surely prefer to enjoy the retiree's freedom in their prime. It should be possible to choose between two options:

Option A:	Option B:
Normal retirement	Pre-work retirement
Work from 20 to 60	Retire from 20 to 40
Retire from 60 until death	Work from 40 until death

Option B would involve a "reverse pension": the financing company would lend young people enough money to live on for twenty years, on the understanding that they would work from 40 until death, and reimburse the loan from their earnings with substantial interest.

ONLINE DATING ASSISTANTS

In French dramatist Rostand's famous play "Cyrano de Bergerac", a clumsy suitor is coached by the more experienced Cyrano, eventually seducing his beloved with the help of Cyrano's chat-up lines. Today when so much dating is conducted over the internet, this could become a reality. Trained "online dating assistants" would be hired by the hour and help strangers charm each other remotely with tried-and-tested techniques.

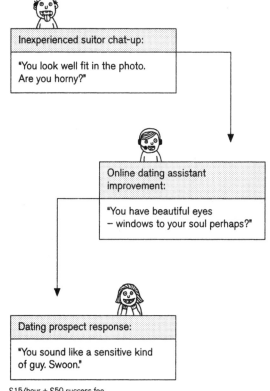

Inexperienced suitor chat-up:

"You look well fit in the photo. Are you horny?"

Online dating assistant improvement:

"You have beautiful eyes – windows to your soul perhaps?"

Dating prospect response:

"You sound like a sensitive kind of guy. Swoon."

£15/hour + £50 success fee

SICK BAGS FOR BINGE-DRINKERS

Binge-drinking is a modern-day scourge yet also a business opportunity. Everyone is familiar with sick bags on planes; they could easily be adapted for the binge-drinking and -vomiting crowd. There are several target markets for this product:

1) Binge-drinkers themselves: throwing up in the street now attracts a £100 fixed penalty fine, which drinkers could easily avoid by going out equipped.

2) Drinking establishments: they would hand out sick bags free at closing time to prevent customers from vomiting all over the neighbourhood and thereby putting their licence at risk.

3) Late-night cab companies: one single incident means removing the cab from circulation for the night and having to clean it thoroughly. This product could save them thousands.

Suggested price: £1/bag

DIGGING: THE SPORT

Digging is an underrated form of exercise, possibly because of its association with graves. Yet it is extremely good for you, easy to learn, and can be great fun. A digging promoter would simply need to rent small plots of land, purchase some spades and a few tons of topsoil, and promote digging as the latest health craze.

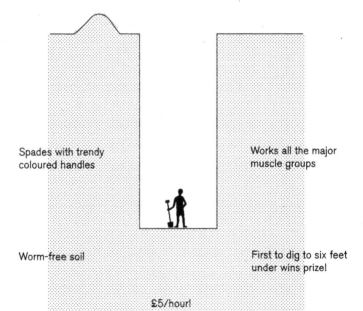

Spades with trendy coloured handles

Works all the major muscle groups

Worm-free soil

First to dig to six feet under wins prize!

£5/hour!

MOTHER'S DAY COMMEMORATIVE UMBILICAL CORD

There is a clear demand for a Mother's Day gift that rises above the crass commercialism of our times, and celebrates the primal mother-child bond with appropriate ceremony. The *Commemorative Umbilical Cord* is the gift for the mother who has everything.

The Commemorative Umbilical Cord celebrates your mother for giving birth to you.

Wear The Commemorative Umbilical Cord on Mother's Day and recreate the sacred link to your mother.

The Commemorative Umbilical Cord clips on to any belt buckle or brooch.

The Commemorative Umbilical Cord is woven from the finest silk, and will last for many Mother's Days ahead!

FAKE WALLETS

Being robbed on holiday can be a nuisance,
even when people have proper travel insurance.
The "fake wallet" solves the problem:
tourists just hand it over and walk away before
the subterfuge is spotted.

(Prototype)

To come with complimentary pull-out phrasebook:	
English	"Put your gun down, here is my wallet!"
French	"Baissez votre pistolet, voici mon portefeuille!"
Spanish	"Baja la pistola, aqui esta mi cartera!"
German	"Nieder mit der Pistole! Hier ist mein Portmonee!"
Italian	"Abassa la pistola! Ecco qui il mio portafoglio!"
Swedish	"Bort med pistolen, här får du min plånbok!"
Croatian	"Spusti pistolj, evo ti moj novcanik!"

JUMP-THE-QUEUE PHONE LINES

Being put on hold in an electronic phone queue is one of life's more stressful experiences. Companies could defuse that stress and earn some extra cash by enabling customers to jump the queue for an appropriate sum e.g. £1. Demo recording:

"...Thank you for calling. All our operators are currently busy with other customers. You are being held in a queue. Your call is important to us and will be answered as soon as possible. Or it will be answered immediately if you press 1 on your phone now, at a cost of £1. Otherwise, please hold for an operator. Your call is important to us and will be answered as soon as possible..."

Some customers may resent the procedure, but they are likely to be poorer and thus less valuable to the company.

PROFESSIONAL SQUATTERS

As most landlords know, the laws against squatting are ridiculously lax. If a dwelling is left unoccupied and squatters break in, they have all sorts of rights that make it very time-consuming and expensive to evict them. "Professional squatters" could occupy empty buildings for a monthly fee, preventing the crustier kind from moving in, and guaranteeing peace of mind for the landlord.

Market size: there are over 700,000 unoccupied homes in the UK. If only 10% of owners were concerned enough about squatters to pay a reasonable £300/month per home, this would put the potential market at over £250 million.

"INVASION IDOL" TV SHOW

This would be an alternative travel show, which involves visiting countries with a view to assessing their suitability for Western invasion – from Iran to Portugal. The reporter would accost local people, from farmers to officials, to smooth the path for the troops. Which field would the farmer prefer we land in? What is the best way to take over the TV station? What historical landmarks should we be careful to preserve?

He would be accompanied by some retired military colonel to take notes and help plan the logistics and invasion routes. At the end of the series, viewers would vote on which foreign country is ripe for invasion, and the results would be delivered to No.10.

"SUCCESSFUL OFFICE" RENTAL PACKAGE

When the Saatchi brothers started their first ad agency in the 70s, they hired actors to populate their office and make potential clients believe they were already hugely successful. In this age of web start-ups, there is enough of a market to make this a viable business model.

This is your lucky day!

Sell! Sell!

That's my last offer!

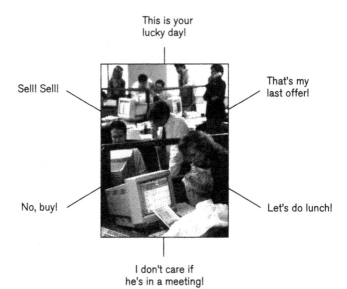

No, buy!

Let's do lunch!

I don't care if he's in a meeting!

For £1,000 a day, the wannabe businessmen would get a dozen pre-trained actors, a buzzing office environment, and an actress PA instructed to interrupt meetings with messages such as "Branson on line one" or "I've cancelled your dinner with the Chancellor".

BIRD-SONG RECOGNIZER

This computerized device would be able to distinguish and recognize different bird sounds from each other, and identify them by name on a little digital screen in the kitchen, along with useful information such as migratory patterns, degree of rarity, and preferred food.

1. Bird in the garden: "Cui-cui"

2. Sound sensor on your kitchen window

YELLOW-CRESTED GREBE
FEMALE OF THE SPECIES
MIGRATING TO AFRICA

3. Computer screen

Suggested retail price: £199.99

INTERNAL COSMETIC SURGERY

True beauty isn't about how you look, it's about what's inside. "Internal cosmetic surgery" would rectify imperfectly-shaped internal organs, so that the cosmetically-enhanced perfection of people's appearance can finally be matched on the inside.

A global chain of clinics would examine people's innards, diagnose any aesthetic malformations, and schedule treatment.

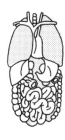

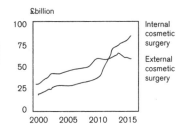

£billion

Internal cosmetic surgery

External cosmetic surgery

"Lopsided Brain"	£9,500
"Untidy Colon"	£7,000
"Ugly Liver"	£5,500
"Misshapen Kidney"	£4,000 each
"Discoloured Rectum"	£3,950

For an extra fee, patients would receive a CAT scan of their improved internal organ to show their friends.

Suggested slogan: Beauty Lies Within

3G VOODOO

The ancient art of voodoo has not yet caught up
with modern technology, which could be used
to make it accessible to a much wider market.
A 3G voodoo application would enable you to
take a photo of your enemy, and send it to a call
centre full of highly-trained voodoo priests in
Haiti, who would curse the enemy for you for a fee.
Examples of curse:

Love rival to
mysteriously
self-combust: £5

Deprive nagging
spouse of power
of speech: £7

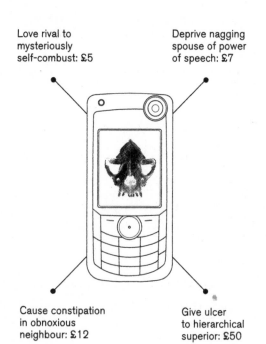

Cause constipation
in obnoxious
neighbour: £12

Give ulcer
to hierarchical
superior: £50

Profit share: 25% to voodoo priest, 25% to you, 50% mobile network charge.

URBAN AQUARIUMS

Aquariums are hugely popular, yet aquarium decoration is stuck in the past. Why should fish swim only through boring castles and other reactionary greenery? Instead, they could swim through modern cityscapes, which would both make their confined lives more exciting, and remind aquarium owners of the potential consequences of global warming and rising sea levels.

Aquarium owners: 3 million (UK only, 2007)
10% share (£50 per cityscape) = £15 million

DEAD-END JOBS AGENCY

Corporations would employ the "dead-end jobs agency" to send their jaded, burnt-out executives to work at truly dire jobs for one week every year, in order to refresh their enthusiasm for their demanding yet well-paid career.

Proper jobs:	Dead-end jobs:
CORPORATE LAWYER	BURGER FLIPPER
Long hours, asshole boss, £350/hour	Long hours, asshole boss, £5.50/hour
ADVERTISING EXECUTIVE	RUBBISH COLLECTOR
Creates rubbish no one wants, £100,000/year	Picks up rubbish no one wants, £10,000/year
ACCOUNTANT	TRAFFIC WARDEN
Doles out bills all day long	Doles out bills all day long, incurring high risk of grievous bodily harm

Corporation pays £5,000 for the one-week reinvigoration course, of which a minimum wage of £220 (£5.50 x 40 hours) goes to the exec, and £4,780 to the agency.

MONEY POOLS

Uncle Scrooge knew how to enjoy his money: by swimming in the stuff. Our affluent times have produced more wealthy individuals than at any point in history, yet most of them are still too busy working to enjoy their money properly. Anyone with assets of over $1,000,000 (certified by their accountant) could visit a "Money Pool" pre-filled with their wealth in one-dollar bills, and bathe in their hard-earned cash for a tiny 0.1% per hour.

$1,000,000+

Small Money Pool

$10,000,000+

Medium Money Pool

$100,000,000+

Olympic Money Pool (Family and friends welcome!)

Also available in pennies for the affluent middle-classes!

CAFÉ IDOL

The purpose of the classic French-style café terrace is to allow idle customers to ogle unsuspecting passers-by and mentally rate their looks. A simple electronic device would make the process both more fun and more scientific: tables could be fitted with a keypad where customers score the passer-by in real time, producing an average which appears under the awning.

No more fruitless philosophical gazing into the middle-distance: the café experience is transformed into an addictive reality show.

SPONSORED HURRICANES

Hurricanes are currently named by the World
Meteorological Organization. Names are
supposedly chosen at random, although they
go through the alphabet (Agatha is followed by
Barbara etc). In 1979, male names were
introduced, after complaints about the association
of natural disasters exclusively with women.
There is a potential opportunity here for corporate
sponsorship, by companies with relevant brand
values. Hurricanes receive worldwide media
coverage, often for weeks. They are synonymous
with two main values: "power" and "danger".

Hurricane "Lucky Strike"

Insurance brands could capitalize on the "danger"
aspect: Hurricane Axa, or Hurricane Zurich
Insurance. Engineering brands would leverage
the "power" connotations: Hurricane Porsche,
or Hurricane Dyson. For this level of media
exposure, brands could expect to pay £1m (higher
if the hurricane is exceptionally strong). 40%
of the profits would go to helping any victims.

CONSUMER NEGOTIATORS

Complaining to a big company isn't always easy.
Contact is usually channelled through call centres,
where staff are taught to deflect any issues and to
take advantage of consumer ignorance of the law.
Instead, consumers could call the negotiator centre
with their details, and the highly-trained negotiator
would then handle the discussion on their behalf,
in exchange for 10% of any money saved as a result.

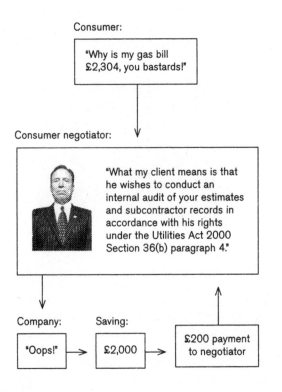

Consumer:

"Why is my gas bill
£2,304, you bastards!"

Consumer negotiator:

"What my client means is that
he wishes to conduct an
internal audit of your estimates
and subcontractor records in
accordance with his rights
under the Utilities Act 2000
Section 36(b) paragraph 4."

Company: Saving:

"Oops!"   →   £2,000   →   £200 payment
                                to negotiator

SUBLIMINAL HYPNOSIS CDs FOR KIDS

Bringing up children is tough, with much that can go wrong. Parents face tremendous anxieties: what if their offspring reject their values? What if they succumb to peer pressure? What if violent video games corrupt them? What if they end up turning to drugs, criminality or prostitution? "Subliminal Hypnosis CDs" enable concerned parents to implant the desired set of beliefs in their children at a very early age, before the conscious mind is even fully-formed; for best results, the CDs should be played to the sleeping toddler every night during the first four years.

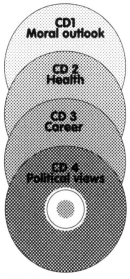

CD Box Set
+ special cot fitted with CD player:

£279.99

"...Hard work is fun...Hard work is rewarding... Homework is especially fun... Delay your gratification... Play hard work hard..."

"...Don't smoke...Smoking is bad...Smoking is for losers...You don't want to get cancer do you now, child?...Smoking is yucky..."

"...Doctor is a fine career... So is lawyer...Artists and actors don't earn any money...They die poor and unhappy...A steady job, that's the ticket..."

"...We live in a free society... The government knows what it's doing...Terrorists are plotting against our way of life...Must watch the evening news..."

"RED PHONE" FOR LOVERS

Like the famous Cold War model that connected the White House and the Kremlin exclusively, this single-button phone would connect people straight through to the most important person in their life.

Manufacture them cheaply in China

One Button Only!

Traditional bakelite finish

Suggested slogan: "Your very own love hotline"

Lockable keypad underneath to program lover's number

TOOTH FAIRY SPONSORSHIP

The tooth fairy is a charming and enduring myth that adds to the magic of growing up. It's also the perfect opportunity for an early marketing push. "Tooth fairy sponsors" could broker deals between parents and child-friendly brands: Lego, for example, could offer a free toy in exchange for each milk tooth.

Milk tooth

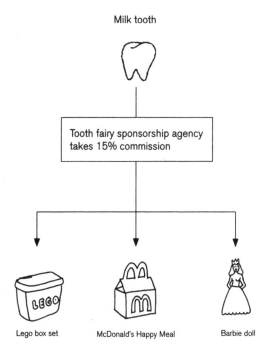

Tooth fairy sponsorship agency takes 15% commission

Lego box set   McDonald's Happy Meal   Barbie doll

This would save the parents money, and establish a lifelong bond between child and brand.

YOUR VERY OWN IDEA

In more culturally elevated days, everyone thought they had a novel in them. Now, it's a business idea. Use the suggestions contained in this book as inspiration to come up with your own ground-breaking masterplan. Then either execute it and become rich, or send it to Benrik for inclusion in any further instalments of this series.

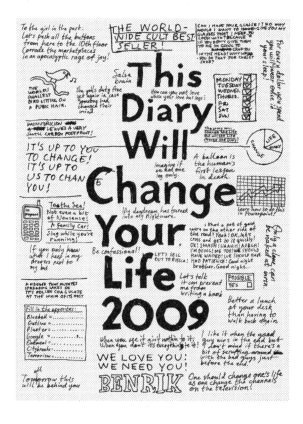

Once you've made your millions, you're
bound to feel spiritually empty, at which
point you'll need the cult bestselling
"This Diary Will Change Your Life",
also by Benrik.

Terms and conditions

You are free to use any of the ideas contained in this book and develop them into multi-million pound businesses, provided you pay Benrik a royalty of 10% on the profits generated (post-tax, to be paid within six months of submission of company's annual accounts, in perpetuity).

Benrik Limited do not take responsibility for any liabilities incurred as a result of the use of their ideas. Readers are urged to seek independent legal and financial advice before attempting to implement Benrik's suggestions.

All ideas may not be valid in all, or any countries. Benrik make no representations, expressed or implied, as to the accuracy of the information and data in this book and accept no liability for any loss or damage caused by inaccurate information.

English law shall apply to any contract within which these terms and conditions are incorporated and you irrevocably agree that the courts of England shall have exclusive jurisdiction to settle any dispute which may arise out of, under, or in connection with these Terms.

Good luck!

Benrik Ltd are Ben Carey and Henrik Delehag.
They were assisted on this project by Claudia Alvear Bello.

The right of Benrik Ltd to be identified as the Author of the Work has been asserted in accordance with the Copyright, Designs and Patents Act 1988.

Many of these ideas first appeared in Benrik's "Free Ideas" column in the *Independent on Sunday* in 2007. Others are long-cherished Benrik projects which they have been pushing on all and sundry for many years in many guises. Benrik thank the following individuals for their help, inspiration or patience: Kathy Peach, Sarah Bagner, Susanne Bagner, Lana Ivanyukhina, Anton Delehag, Dusty Miller, Tim Lewis, Simon Trewin, Ariella Feiner, Jon Butler, Bruno Vincent, Richard Milner, Rebecca Ikin, Amy Lines, James Long, Euan Adie, Michael Bhaskar, Sara Lloyd, Alex Rayner, Richard Hytner, Bernard David, Robert Saville, Matt Clark and all at Mother, Igor Clark and all at Poke, Eleanor Roome, Ollie Wright, Hannah, Carol MacArthur, Hayley Newman, Andy Moreno, Jon Cooke, Trevor Franklin, Simon Lai, Richard Prue Alex & Elizabeth Carey, Aunt, Katy Follain, Antony Topping, Stefanie, Charlotte, Tommy and Matty Drews, Colin Rowat, Gaby Vinader, Sarah Woodruff, Tom Uhart, Alan Payne, Jan Lyness, Bernard Sue & John Peach, Fredrik Nordbeck, Eva Edsjö, Alex Hutchins, Rina Donnersmarck, Almut, Kenneth & Anna-Lena & Lovisa & Hjalmar & Elin Delehag.

www.benrik.co.uk

All illustrations, photography, design and typography by Benrik, except as follows. The authors would like to gratefully thank for permission to include the following within this edition: photography ideas 9, 17 (car), 22, 37, 38, 56, 66, 67, 72, 75 (spider, sick), 94, 99, 101, 102, 108, 115, 124, 125, 138, 146, 147 © Getty Images. Photography idea 83 © PA Photos. Photography idea 75 (larvae) © Benjamin Harink. Photography used under the terms of the Creative Commons Public Licence, which can be found on Flickr: idea 5 "Brick Lane" (fotologic); idea 22 "Me on the phone" (Ironiclvy / Ivy VanZanten); idea 25 "Liverpool Street station crowd blur" (victoriapeckham / David Sim); idea 33 "Skull eye" (Jon Hurd / Laertes); idea 53 "Silo" (Plano Light / Bill Cunningham); idea 57 "Portland Vase" (Jorge-11); idea 61 "Barbed Adidas" (dogbomb / Simon Brass); idea 63 "London northern line tube" (Mark Hillary); idea 110 "happy cows come from California" (Lin Pernille), "An umbrella for my convertible" (Damouns / Damien Boilley), "Windsurfing" (Joe Shlabotnik); idea 118 "JOH_5789" star5112 (wine); idea 139 "Bird song" (aussiegall); idea 142 "NYC Twin Towers" (badlogik). In the spirit of reciprocity, any of these Flickr photographers who wants one can receive a free copy of this book. Idea 51 © Justin Dorey. Idea 46 © Paul Drew. Idea 5 © Sarah Bagner. Idea 92 © Alex Hutchins. If there is further enquiry, please contact the authors c/o Macmillan, 20 New Wharf Road, London N1 9RR.

First published 2008 by Boxtree
An imprint of Pan Macmillan Ltd
Pan Macmillan, 20 New Wharf Road, London N1 9RR
Basingstoke and Oxford
Associated companies throughout the world
www.panmacmillan.com

ISBN 978-0-7522-2670-5

9 8 7 6 5 4 3 2 1

A CIP catalogue record for this book is available from the British Library

Printed and bound in the UK by CPI Mackays, Chatham ME5 8TD

Benrik Limited

Visit www.benrik.co.uk
for updates on which ideas
are being developed.